BEULAH MEIER PELTON

WE BELONG
TO THE LAND

Memories of a Midwesterner

BEULAH MEIER PELTON

IOWA STATE UNIVERSITY PRESS
Ames, Iowa

For my sons
DON, BILL, and JIM
and their father, now gone

Drawings by Bob Artley

Composed and printed by The Iowa State University Press,
Ames, Iowa 50010

First edition, 1984

Library of Congress Cataloging in Publication Data

Pelton, Beulah Meier, 1914–
    We belong to the land.

    1. Pelton, Beulah Meier, 1914–   . 2. Farm life – Iowa. 3. Iowa – Social life and customs.
4. Pelton family. 5. Iowa – Biography. I, Title.
CT275.P5523A39   1984   977.7′032′0922   84–10913
ISBN 0–8138–1143–0

Contents

Foreword

I have served on the Manuscript Committee for the Iowa State University Press for twenty-plus years. During that time I have read literally hundreds of manuscripts.

Of its kind, this book, *We Belong to the Land,* is the best I've ever read. Not only is it written with great sensitivity but it provides a deep insight into the relationship of man to land that can only be appreciated by someone who has been there.

Beulah Meier Pelton was there. She happened to be there before the onrush of farm technology brought comforts and conveniences to most farm homes that were beyond the imagination of those who survived the depression years—the depression of the Thirties. But this story is not dated. Mrs. Pelton speaks of "loving the land" and having faith that "the land will not fail. If one year is bad, there is always the chance that the next year will be better." Readers now, or at any time, will have a better appreciation of where farmers are "coming from" and what makes them who they are and like they are after finishing this book. You will taste, smell, and feel every facet of this Iowa farm story, and you will enjoy every minute of it.

Well, no, there *are* some tears; and the first you will shed is when the author describes her father coming home to tell the family—amidst his own tears—that all is lost. "It's all gone— the farm, livestock, everything." The mortgage was foreclosed.

So, devastated and despondent, the family moves to town—as they always do. But later, the author, now grown, marries and moves back to a farm; for some this is where the story really begins. For this farm wife then experiences the grinding hardships that were the lot of farm families (and particularly farm wives) before any of today's modern conveniences. But the author tells the story with such verve and self-deprecating humor that there are smiles and love and basic satisfactions amidst the heartaches and the drudgery.

Thomas Jefferson would have loved this book; this was the rural America that he envisaged as he gazed westward; people of the land, loving farm life. You will enjoy this book too.

There is another book of a similar nature that covers this same period of our rural history. Its title is *In No Time At All,* and it came from my own typewriter. My mother, as might be expected, was embarrassingly proud of that effort. She would never ever admit to any flaws in the effort. With some wistfulness, however, she would occasionally remark that "of course, the book was written from a man's point of view."

My mother would have loved this book—as you surely will—not only because it is written from a woman's point of view but also because it is a beautifully written story that pictures a period of rural American history better than any other single book you may have an opportunity to read.

CARL HAMILTON

Preface

We Belong to the Land is the result of my long-cherished belief that somebody ought to write a book about real, honest-to-God, down-on-the-farm farmers. I don't think it has been done before.

To be sure, there are people who buy four or five acres of land, turn a romantic old barn into a delightful home, acquire a milk cow with a fancy name, and then write glowingly about the joys of country living. Although I read of their experiences with pleasure, I do not consider these people to be farmers.

When I speak of farmers I mean people who turn the soil, sow the crops, and reap the harvest — people who have no source of income other than the farm, people who belong to the land. They are broad-shouldered people, men of hard sinew and callused hands and women of courage and quiet determination. They are the people who go about the business of feeding a goodly portion of the world.

This book is the story of one such farm family and of some of the generations that preceded it.

WE BELONG TO THE LAND

Mother's People

IT was a yearning for land that brought my mother's people to Iowa in 1848. Little is remembered now of that first generation, except that they came from Holland. But no one thought it important to pass along the information as to exactly when they came to America, nor how long they lived in this country before they decided to come to Iowa.

They came to Harrison County in a covered wagon. At that time they must have been squatters, for no surveying was done before 1852 on the rich bottomlands along the Missouri River where they chose to make their home.

However, my mother adamantly refused to call her people "squatters," a term which implied improvidence and shiftlessness to her. She insisted on calling them "pioneers" or "early settlers." My mother was proud of her relatives and regaled us with stories about them until she died at the age of ninety-nine. She was sure that they were the most courageous and resourceful settlers ever to come to the prairies. And I like to think she was right. Out of pride in my ancestry and a desire to feel that some of the same staunch pioneer blood runs in my veins—I want to think that she was right.

It was Evalina, the oldest daughter in the family of these early arrivals, who grew up to become my grandmother, and it was she who became the heroine of the stories my mother used to tell. When I was a child, Evalina was so very old and wrinkled and fragile that she looked like a good stiff wind could have blown her away. Her hair was cotton-white and had been that way since she was in her thirties. In the callowness of my youth I could never imagine her smooth of cheek, with a spring in her step and romance in her heart. I suppose I must have been thinking along these lines that summer day when she and I were sitting in the porch swing at the rambling house where she spent her long widowhood.

"Grandma," I asked, "how long have you been old?"

"Gracious sakes, child, what an odd question!" she answered. "Don't you know you'll be old yourself someday?"

"Well, I suppose so," I said, somewhat uncomfortably, sensing that I might have overstepped my bounds with the question. I decided to use a different tack.

"Do you remember being young?" I inquired.

"Of course, I remember being young. I remember everything about it."

"How long did it last?" I probed.

"Not very long. I grew up fast. I was married at sixteen and had my first young'un when I was seventeen."

"Did the other girls get married at sixteen?"

"Most of them did. In those days people used to think that a girl of sixteen or even younger was old enough to get married and have a family of her own. As soon as I saw your grandfather I knew he was the man for me and there wasn't any need to wait."

Grandpa Jacob Lightell did not come to Iowa in the relative comfort of a prairie schooner, as Evalina had done. He was but a lad in Ohio when his mother died. She had been a good woman, a gentle woman who stood between her children and their stern father and, after her death, Jacob found life with his father impossible. Without telling anyone in the family what he intended to do, he hired on as a cattle driver with a wagon train and he walked every step of the way to Iowa. The year was 1860.

We do not know where Grandpa met Evalina. Perhaps it was at church, because everybody socialized by going to church in those days. Or perhaps it was at one of the dances where the men—smelling of tobacco and corn liquor—and the women—with the merest hint of twin petticoats peeping out from under the ruffled skirts of their turkey red or bright blue calico—do-si-doed the night away to the cajoling whine of a red-hot fiddle. Wherever it was, the first time Evalina saw Jacob he was wearing a pair of trousers he had made himself. Times were hard then, and cloth, even when it was available, was too expensive to buy. So he had used the only material available to him — gunny sacks. A double layer of gunny cloth whipped together with twine produced a garment that covered him quite adequately, although they pricked unmercifully in hot weather. In later years, Evalina would chuckle over these gunny sack pants. But no matter. Jacob was tall and dark and rakishly handsome and she fell in love with him anyway.

Their first home was a log cabin on the bottomlands not far from the Missouri River. Evalina was lucky to have a cabin and she knew it, for there were many families living in dugouts in the hills with only a blanket to hang over the doorway to keep out the cold and the mosquitoes. So she tore into the cabin with sprightly energy and made a home out of it.

She knew how to do everything — make candles, make lye out of wood ashes, make her own soap, and make hominy from field corn. She wove her own linen out of homegrown flax.

Color in one's home was important, of course, and Evalina knew how to get it. For the blues, reds, and purples, she boiled wild berries until she got the intensity she wanted. If she needed a sunny yellow, she knew how to get that, too. She merely dipped her cloth into something that was always plentiful — human urine. This practice may seem preposterous to the reader. However, it was commonly done in those days. Evalina told my mother about it; she later told me. I made inquiries and found that many people have heard the same story from older members of their families. She was careful that all her linens had a good washing, however. To do this she took them to the creek, rubbed her homemade soap on the spots, and used a stone for a washboard.

At first she baked her bread by wrapping the dough around a stick and holding it over the fire. Jacob, seeing that Evalina got roasted right along with her bread, made a metal spit for her, something she could use in the fireplace in the winter or over an open fire in the summer.

Meanwhile, Jacob yoked up his oxen and broke the virgin prairie for his first crop. When it came time to plant corn he made holes with a hoe while Evalina followed him, carrying the seed in her apron and dropping it into the ground. Jacob had to scurry around behind her and cover it up quickly, before the prairie chickens could get to it.

The patient oxen were much more practical than horses in those days, for the horses were so tortured by flies and mosquitoes that it was almost impossible for a man to hold them to a furrow. There were always new settlers coming in who needed plowing done, so Jacob became a sort of entrepreneur. He bought several span of oxen and hired them and himself out to break the stubborn prairie sod.

There were no large forests on the bottomlands but there were straight-limbed cottonwoods, sprawling oaks, rough-barked elder, ash, and walnut trees — all good cabin, barn, fence, and fireplace woods. However, it was difficult to get to the trees for they stood among thickets of tough willow, sumac, wild roses, bittersweet, and rosen weed so tangled that a man could scarcely force his way through them.

Yet these thickets held great rewards for there could be found the fruits and berries that broke the pioneers' monotonous diet. In the spring strawberries grew plump and rosy. In the summer tart gooseberries could be stripped off by the handfuls from their prickly bushes and clusters of wild grapes dangled from vines that clung tenaciously to everything within reach. In the autumn the stocky plum trees bore their orange-purple fruit and honey could be taken by the kegful.

There were many Indians on the prairies then; no large tribes, but segments of tribes whose homes were elsewhere. Small bands of Sioux, Pottawatamies, and Omahas wandered in and out of the territory at will, camping for weeks and sometimes months while they hunted deer or elk or speared the ubiquitous beaver. Once each year the Winnebagoes came to fish for carp and pickerel and the huge channel "cat" in the large lakes that had been formed out of the overflow of the Missouri River.

The Indians often came to Evalina's cabin to beg for food. Usually she tried to talk them out of it. If the Indians refused to leave she gave them as little out of her precious larder as she dared. As she told us many years later, those Indians' knives looked awfully sharp and she knew when to back down.

To the end of her days, Evalina would remember the freshly baked plum pie that the Indians stole from her. She had set it out on the porch to cool, and when she went to get it, it was gone. She knew where it went, for a half dozen Indians were riding down the road on their spotted ponies, and they were grubbing the pie out of the pan with their hands.

Evalina stayed at the cabin alone with her first child while Jacob went away to the Civil War for a year. She was just a girl of seventeen but she was also a married woman, and she had no desire to go back to her parents' home and make a burden of herself. It was a lonely time for her but she managed quite well. However, once she dallied too long when the Missouri River flooded and she had to walk in water up to her arms to get herself and her baby to safety. In later years, she talked about this only when she was asked, and she never seemed to attach too much importance to this awesome exploit. It was just something that had to be done and she did it.

It was the same way with crossing the river on the ice. Evalina's young brother, Pete, lived in Nebraska. She was fond of him and they often went to see him. Summer was no time to go, for crossing that treacherous river in a small boat would have been foolhardy at best, even if they had had a boat. So they made these crossings in the winter when the river was frozen over.

However, they had a system for this: each person had two planks. The first was laid down to walk on while you carried the second. You walked to the end of the first plank, and laid the second down to step on. Then you turned around and picked up your first plank and carried it until you needed it. This system worked if you didn't wait until the ice had begun to break up in the spring, or if you didn't get out in the middle of the river and lose your nerve and start screaming for help.

Jacob and Evalina made several of these trips in the early years of their married life, but my grandmother did not seem to think that they had shown any particular bravery when they made these crossings. They had merely wanted to visit Uncle Pete and his family and had taken the shortest, easiest route open to them.

Through all these years Evalina's children just kept coming—eleven of them. "Young'uns," she called them. I never heard her refer to her own or to anyone else's children by any term other than young'uns. She raised eight to adulthood, which was a pretty good batting average for a woman of her day.

With so many children, it was inevitable that there be illnesses. But Evalina always started doctoring before things got out of hand, and she had her own remedies for just about everything. Goose grease or lard melted together with turpentine and applied to young chests under several thicknesses of heated flannel was her standard treatment for colds and influenza (they called it "grippe") and what was no doubt pneumonia sometimes. Sumac syrup soothed sore throats and, if you felt feverish, the thing to do was take massive doses of quinine and go to bed.

Once, when her 12-year-old son Charlie cut an artery in his arm and blood spurted to the ceiling, Evalina did not panic. She worked for hours with the boy, applying a mixture of sugar and soap under his bandages, although what possible connection there is between sugar and soap and severed arteries I cannot imagine. But she got the bleeding stopped and Charlie lived until he was in his late eighties.

Nobody knew about germs, but Evalina was scrupulously clean about the house. No doubt she used enough of her homemade lye soap to kill a lot of germs. However, her children attended school where the water pail was passed along the rows of desks, and the pupils all drank from the same dipper. My mother was so appalled by this lack of cleanliness in school that she never got thirsty unless she was at home.

The pioneers knew that smallpox was contagious, but they seem to have had no inkling as to the source of typhoid. Evalina's older brother took his bride to a house where there had been several deaths the year before, probably due to contaminated well water. Within the month she was dead and he was very ill. Evalina sent Jacob after him and she nursed him back to health at their cabin.

The pioneers had a signal they used when someone had died of a contagious disease. They nailed a long pole with a white flag at the top on their house or barn; then they waited for neighbors to notice their signal. If they lived in an out-of-the-way place, or if no one knew there was illness in the family, it might be several days before anyone came to help.

To lose a beloved child and not even be able to have a funeral or see to the burial must have been an agonizing experience, but it happened to my grandparents in 1869, when they lost their three-year-old son George to smallpox. Jacob built the casket with his own hands and Evalina lined it with her softest quilt. Then he carried the casket out and set it on top of the woodpile, put up the long pole with the white flag on it — and they waited.

Coming after the body of someone who had died from a contagious disease took a special kind of courage, and the bereaved family thereafter had a deep feeling of gratefulness for the people who performed this duty. So it was with Evalina who, when she was very old, still spoke fondly of the men who had come for her young son that day.

With doctors hard to come by and with Evalina having had all those young'uns herself, it was natural that she be called upon to midwife sometimes. My mother always remembered how Evalina would come home flushed with victory when the birth was successful and her sorrow when it wasn't.

Evalina's burgeoning brood soon overflowed the cabin, of course, so Jacob built a new frame house for her — one with an upstairs like the town women had. He found that he was good at carpentry and soon he was building houses for other people. Two of them are still standing on a high hill that overlooks the flatlands where he once broke the prairie sod with oxen. One of the houses is falling down from neglect, the other still in use after more than a century.

Evalina's family of brothers and sisters were soon scattered, but the railroad enabled them to visit occasionally. It was Evalina's sister Hetty, who lived in Kansas but came to Iowa once a year, that became the unwitting pivot for a strange series of comic and near tragic events.

Although Hetty had been married twice she was widowed both times, and she was still childless when she was in her late thirties. Evalina, who had spent eight and a quarter years — give or take a few weeks either way — being pregnant, couldn't understand it.

And it wasn't that Hetty didn't try, either. After a decent period of mourning for her second husband, she got married again. Meanwhile, she wasn't getting any younger, and I suppose it was inevitable that her taste in husbands become less discriminating as the years went by. At any rate, it was when she brought her third husband back to Iowa that Evalina realized Hetty was going to strike out again. The reason was quite evident—she couldn't get husband number three to come to bed. No matter how much she coaxed or how often Jacob and Evalina protested the unseemliness of the situation, he refused to come to bed. Day after day, night after night, he sat in a rocking chair by the window where he could watch the road. He didn't undress and even refused to take his boots off.

Evalina was disgusted and thought that Hetty should have been able to do better than marry a man like that. Jacob conceded that he was a queer one and that a man who wouldn't take his eyes off the road was either running from the law or some old enemies. It was this uneasy feeling that may have saved Jacob and his family from a terrible death.

Hetty and her husband had been given the spacious downstairs bedroom for their visit; while Jacob and Evalina and their brood slept upstairs. One night Jacob was awakened by a feeling of premonition, some sixth sense warning him that all was not well within his household. He could see a light burning in the kitchen and, very quietly, he arose and went downstairs. He saw Hetty's husband sitting detached and motionless at the kitchen table, staring into space as if his thoughts were far away. Jacob circled cautiously around the man and saw that he had an axe leaning against his chair, his hand on the handle. Jacob snatched the axe, took it to the woodshed, and stayed on guard the remainder of the night.

When Hetty came to breakfast the next morning, Jacob explained the situation to her and suggested that it might be a good idea if she took her husband back to Kansas. She accepted the suggestion without rancor and they left on the next train.

Nobody was ever sure what Three intended to do with that axe, but Jacob believed to the end of his days that the man intended to kill them all in their sleep—and probably wouldn't have known whom he was killing nor why he was doing it.

Hetty was devoted to Jacob and Evalina and she continued to write regularly. Once day a letter arrived saying, not uncheerfully, that Three had simply sat down in his chair and died—presumably with his boots on. After this Hetty began to make her yearly visits to Iowa again, her two trunks loaded with finery, for one of her husbands had been rich and she could afford to indulge herself. If she ever knew what awesome terrors had possessed Three's mind, she never told anybody.

Evalina loved her sister, of course, but I know it irked her the way Hetty flaunted her nice clothes and her jewelry and never offered to help with the housework or the dishes. Hetty could sit for hours with her soft, white hands in her lap so that her rings would show, while Evalina worked circles around her. Evalina would try to act as if this didn't bother her, but toward the end of Hetty's visit she would always be clattering the dishes and rattling the pans a little louder. At least that is how I remember it as a child. After three or four weeks I could sense the tension in my grandmother's house, and then I knew it was time for Hetty to go back to Kansas again.

It took a prodigious effort just to keep food on the table for a family the size of Jacob's and Evalina's. So he used to supplement their larder by trapping wild turkeys. He always took his rifle when he went out to check his traps, and if it hadn't been for that rifle he would have disappeared one day without a trace. There was often quicksand along the edges of the harmless-looking prairie streams — treacherous stuff that could suck a man in very quickly. It did no good to struggle, for that just made the quicksand work all the faster and, in a few minutes, it would all be over.

Jacob was aware of this danger, of course, but the ground must have looked solid enough to him or else he had his mind on something else at the time. He took that next and almost fatal step and suddenly felt his feet sinking down and out from under him. His rifle was in the clear, however, and he laid it across the quicksand to help support his weight while he looked around for something to catch hold of. He saw a willow branch no larger than a child's finger hanging over his head. Very carefully, so as not to activate the quicksand, he reached up and grabbed it. Mercifully, the tough willow held, and he was able to pull himself to safety.

Evalina was not one to let a dinner on the wing get away from her. One day she saw three prairie hens sitting close together on a fence. She ran for the shotgun, took aim, and whaled away — killing all three birds with one blast of the gun. I think she was prouder of killing those prairie chickens than she was of anything she ever did in her life and, in later years, any allusion to this story always brought an amused chuckle from her.

My mother always said that Evalina was an indifferent cook, but with all those young'uns it is hard to see how she could have had the time and inclination for cooking anything but the plainest foods. But even when she was in her nineties she could make noodles that far surpassed anything the other women in the family could make.

Ah! Those noodles! I can remember them yet, golden with egg and dusty with flour, rolled out into big sheets and hanging over the backs of chairs on clean tea towels until such time as they were deemed proper for cutting. I, already a too-plump child who should not have been allowed within thirty miles of a noodle, would eat them until I was ready to burst.

Evalina's big kitchen was a delightful place to me—not only because of the noodles—important though they were—but also because of her canaries, over which she did a great deal of fussing. In the fall she shook hemp seeds (known today as marijuana) into a sheet and brought them back for her birds. Small wonder her canaries sang!

The female Betsy occasionally laid eggs and hatched little ones, although I don't think she was very good at that because there always seemed to be a long wait between hatches, and Evalina was continually putting different nesting material in the cage or trying out some new kind of cuttlebone in an effort to bring Betsy around. More often than not, she did not respond.

But it was a great day when she did lay an egg. Evalina was almost as proud of that egg as if she had produced it herself—and I couldn't keep my nose out of the cage. Evalina would tell me sternly to get away from there because no canary would put up with any "botherment" while she was laying and if I even so much as breathed on that egg, Betsy would never sit on it again. So I would wait until Evalina had left the room, and then I would sneak back for another look. It wasn't that I meant to be disobedient. I just couldn't stay away from that cage and that egg. I must have been responsible for an awful lot of canary abortions.

I was never able to call Jacob "Grandfather," because he died long before I was born. But I had Evalina for a grandmother until long after I was grown up and married. She was as wrinkled then as a white raisin and there was a large, pink bald spot on top of her head. A mass of blue veins coursed under the skin on those hands that had once been so busy, and the blue eyes that had seen so much were faded and rheumy behind her spectacles. She had never been very big, but all those years of childbearing had left her with a bulge she could not hide, and she looked pregnant to the end of her days.

During the last few years, her eyesight failed and she could no longer do the colorful embroidery or make the softly textured quilts in which she had once taken so much pride. However, she still took pride in her appearance. She wore high-laced black shoes that gleamed with polish. Invariably, a starched, rickrack trimmed apron covered her long-sleeved, rickracky dress.

In the summers she spent hours sitting in her porch swing, watching up the dusty street of the small town where nothing ever seemed to happen. These were the times when she was most receptive to my questions. All her young'uns and their young'uns had heard her stories. But I hadn't. I was the youngest one and I was like a blank sheet of paper waiting to be written on. I think—I hope—that she enjoyed me.

So Evalina has always meant a lot of little things to me, things like noodles and canaries and pointy-toed shoes. And, she has meant a lot of big things to me, too, like carrying little Charlie through the flood and birthing all those babies and facing up to those Indians and their long knives.

So it was with Ma's folks, who came to Iowa in a Conestoga or walked fifteen hundred miles to get here, who rode horseback twenty miles each way to get their mail, fought in the Civil War, survived a flood, a couple of grasshopper plagues, the blizzard of '88, broke virgin sod with oxen, and lived among Indians.

My mother always said that her people survived all those hard years only because they were innovative, and ambitious, and had lots of courage.

But it always seemed to me that they had a disproportionate share of good luck, too. What would have happened, for instance, if that little sapling hadn't been right above Jacob's head when he fell into the quicksand? What would have happened if he had not wakened in time to stop Aunt Hetty's husband from using that axe? And what would have happened if the ice had given way and Jacob and Evalina had gone to their deaths in the Missouri River?

It's pretty hard to figure these things out. But it does look like there wouldn't have been any me.

Father's People, My People

M Y brother Don, sister Gladys, and I grew up thinking that Mother's people were the most heroic men and women ever to come to Iowa. But with my father's family it was different. They came to this country too late to be considered pioneers, and by the time they arrived most of the prairie had been plowed, most of the Indians had been banished to reservations, and almost nobody lived in log cabins anymore.

Furthermore, none of Dad's people were heroes and they didn't want to be heroes. They even left their native land so that nobody would be tempted to make heroes out of them. All they wanted to do was live out their lives in peace. They were sick of Europe's endless wars that sapped the health and lifeblood out of their men. It wasn't that they were pacifists in any true sense of the word. They just didn't want to fight.

So in 1868, with the wily Bismarck once more bringing the political pot to a boil, they booked passage on a boat for America and left Schleswig-Holstein behind forever. Both sets of my paternal grandparents came over on the same boat, although the two families did not know each other. My grandparents were four years old at the time. It was many years later, after Mary Schultz and Henry Meier (the name had been Swartzmeier in Germany) grew up and fell in love, that they found out they had made the crossing together.

Most of the passengers were sturdy peasant people and they had planned the trip to America for a long time. They mourned the families they had left behind and would most likely never see again, but they prayed that they would reach land safely and that the New World would be good to them.

But the Atlantic seas were rough and dangerous and the crossing took many weeks. Inevitably, some passengers did not survive. My grandmother's young brother died on the way and was buried at sea. I do not know the name of this child nor how old he was. My information about him is sketchy, either because Grandmother didn't know the details or because they were lost in the transition from one generation to another. The burial at sea, if my grandmother was allowed to witness it, must have been a very traumatic experience for a child of four, and maybe that is why she didn't talk very much about it. My great grand-parents anguished over their lost child. But who could say that he would not have died had they never left Germany? The Germans have a saying: if it is your time to go, Death will find you no matter where you are.

The Schultzes lived in Chicago at first and my grand-mother worked there as a dairy maid when she was in her teens. But it was land they wanted. Ah, the land! There had never been enough of it in the Old Country. But here in America there was plenty. So their next move was to Northeast Iowa, already a haven for German immigrants. And it was here that short, brown-eyed Mary met and fell in love with tall, blue-eyed Henry.

Grandpa was all for getting married at once, but Grand-ma's cooler head prevailed. First, she said, they would have to get some money saved up. They both worked hard and saved every cent they could, but the money did not seem to pile up very fast. Then, almost a year after they had decided to get married, they were offered live-in jobs on the same farm. Grandpa was to work in the fields while Grandma was to work in the house and milk the cows. In 1880 that seemed like a golden opportunity! Now they could be married and not have the expense of keeping up a household.

Grandma was ambitious and dutiful and she milked those cows no matter what. My father always liked to tell how, when he was about to come into this world, he was out with his mother getting the cows in. She barely made it back to the house in time to give birth to the first of her three sons.

Three years after my father Albert's birth, my grandparents had enough money saved up to make a down payment on forty acres of their own. And just in time, too, for they had another baby coming and they yearned for a home of their own.

Neither one of them ever saw the inside of a schoolhouse as a student. I never saw Grandpa read nor write, although he was alert and seemed intelligent. But with Grandma it was different. She wanted an education desperately and when my father started to school she saw her chance. When he came home from school he sat down at his mother's side and taught her what he had learned that day. She was an apt pupil and could soon read and write. Later on, she bought a typewriter and learned to use it.

Henry believed that a man was put on this earth to work hard and earn money, and that when he got his hands on the money, he would be a fool to part with it. I suppose that my grandmother must have had much the same philosophy, otherwise she would have found life with him impossible. This obsession to conserve every penny became more important to them than pleasure, health, or even family—as we were to find out some years later.

"Safing," they called it, and it was a word they used often. But all their "safing" paid off, for they practically leapfrogged to prosperity. When they had their first forty acres paid for they bought forty more to put with it. When that was paid for they sold it and bought a hundred and sixty.

But this was not without cost. My father often recalled the austerity of his parents' home. A gallon of kerosene was made to last a year in their lamp. Leather shoes were precious and not to be worn unless absolutely necessary. He remembered herding cattle by the roadside when sharp, frozen clods cut his feet until they bled. At home he and his brothers wore knitted house boots that Grandma made out of yarn she had spun herself, the fleece for it having come from the scrapings the sheep had left on the fences. When the children went to school they crept off by themselves to eat so that the other pupils would not see what they had—which was always homemade bread spread with lard or molasses that soaked through in warm weather and froze in the winter. A banana or an orange was a rare treat, to be enjoyed only at Christmastime.

Nor was this all. When my father was twelve, his parents "hired" him out for ten dollars a month to a farmer who lived some fifteen miles away. The farmer had seen my father in church, you see, and had thought he looked sturdy enough to do a man's work. My father was not consulted; he was in school when the decision was made. When he came home and found out what had been done, he felt betrayed, as indeed he was. He was an excellent student and wanted to stay in school.

My grandparents were in their early forties when they rented the farm to my father and moved to town, where they built a fine, new house big enough for roomers. Grandpa, this German immigrant who could neither read nor write, became a part of an educational system for the first time in his life. He got a job janitoring at the local school. In the winter he was continually fussed up over his boilers. Grandpa and Grandma arose at four and breakfasted hastily. Then he went off to stoke the furnaces at the school while she read her Bible, pieced quilts, and waited impatiently for the roomers to get out of their beds. At ten he came home for a second breakfast, usually homemade bread and summer sausage, spiced with hot, black peppercorns. Afterwards he hurried back to school before one of his recalcitrant boilers got too hot.

All this work and heavy food seemed to be good for Grandpa. He stayed straight and tall and walked with the loose-limbed stride of a youth. But the homemade bread and summer sausage played cruel tricks on Grandma over the years, until she became almost as broad as she was tall. Some unlucky whale had given his all for her corset, but it was impossible to subtract more than an inch or two from that ample girth, and a lot of the real Grandma continued to bubble out wherever the whale left off.

Nobody ever talked about dieting in those days and I'm not too sure they even understood the relationship of diet to weight. Everybody cheerfully ate and enjoyed themselves, and people like Grandma just kept cinching up their corsets. Happiness was equated with eating exactly what you wanted and all you wanted. Anyway, it would have been hard to convince us that there was a connection between eating fatty foods and being overweight because we had proof to the contrary right in the family. Grandpa not only ate fried side pork, summer sausage, and homemade bread with gravy over it, but he also drank cream straight from the pitcher. And he never gained an ounce.

Whenever we ate at their big, round table he always finished the meal with the same ritual. His long arm would reach out and grab the cream pitcher, which he would pass around the table under our very noses, saying, "Does anybody want this cream? If you don't I'll drink it."

And down the hatch it would go.

We didn't eat at that big, round table very often, for Grandma was no hand to ask "company" in. But sometimes we would drop in on her when it was near meal time and then she would ask us to stay. Almost always the meal would be stew. She opened a quart each of home-canned meat, tomatoes, peas, and green beans, and dumped it all together in a big kettle. Then she would add some potatoes and let the whole thing simmer for an hour. It served seven people, and it was delicious, and hadn't cost her a dime out of pocket.

My mother was always on the defensive about her relatives and we had to keep a civil lip when we talked about them. But my father didn't have any heroes to defend, and we were allowed to be amused by his relatives and their peculiarities.

Dad's Uncle Ambrose and Aunt Mathilda lived on the banks of the Wapsipinicon River some fifteen miles away and we children loved to visit them because there was a sandy beach a few yards from the house where we could go swimming. Aunt Mathilda thought it was dangerous for us to swim in the "Wapsi," but when she saw that we were going to do it anyway, she would come out on her back porch and yell, "You kids watch out for them leeches and them water moccasins now!" Then, after having done her duty and given us fair warning, she would go back into the house, slamming the screen door loudly behind herself.

Water moccasins and leeches we could handle. But we always had a healthy respect for Aunt Mathilda's two bulldogs—huge, scowling, ill-tempered beasts with jaws that hung down like hams and ears that were always covered with axle grease in the summer to keep the flies off. The dogs would lie panting in the hot sun, sometimes under a shade tree but more often in front of the kitchen door, from which spot they could be dislodged only by a great deal of yelling and fond cursing. They had absolutely no energy at all. A rabbit could have run across their noses without causing any diminution in their torpidity. They seemed utterly useless to anyone who didn't love them.

But Aunt Mathilda was devoted to her dogs and used to tell us how viciously they fought, and how they sometimes fastened together in a death grip so terrible that she would have to pry their jaws apart with a spade. She related these stories with such pride that you knew she thought any two beasts who didn't fight so hard you had to pry them apart with a spade, simply weren't worth their salt in bulldoggery.

At least fifty percent of Uncle Ambrose's vocabulary consisted of swear words that rolled off his tongue as innocently as the mouthings of a nursery rhyme from a three year old. His swearing was just a habit that didn't mean anything and, deep down, he was just as religious as anybody.

Once, when we were at their house for a picnic dinner, we were all seated around the long table under the trees. After Aunt Mathilda had kicked the bulldogs out from under the table and things had gotten quieted down, Uncle Ambrose looked around solemnly and, no doubt thinking it was time to call on a higher power, turned to his wife and demanded, "By God, Mathilda—you pray!"

Mathilda prayed.

Uncle Ambrose and Aunt Mathilda had lots of money, and not being ones to trust them "sonsabitchen bankers in them sonsabitchen banks," they buried their money out in the back yard in cream cans. Once, when they had bought another farm and the seller was there waiting for his money, Uncle Ambrose sent Aunt Mathilda out to dig up one of these cream cans. Dutifully, she came lugging it in. Uncle Ambrose took one look at it and said, "Kee-rist, Mathilda, you got the wrong can!" So she took that can back and buried it and dug up another one.

No thief ever tried to steal one of those cream cans. And it was just as well. The bulldogs probably would have taken a leg off anyone who tried it, and Aunt Mathilda probably would have cheered them on.

So my father's people had two things going for them—religion and money. When it came to religion, my Grandmother Meier covered all bases. She was a devout Methodist, admired Catholicism, and befriended a Jewish peddler, whose name was Goldberg. He walked through the countryside with a pack on his back selling whatever small items he could to the farm wives. Grandma's other roomers paid, of course. But never Goldberg. He was allowed to sleep for free on her porch any time he came to the little town of Fredericksburg, Iowa. Sometimes he baked an egg overnight in the warm ashes of the kitchen stove, and this would be his breakfast.

There were a few years of prosperity for farmers during and after World War I, and this is when my father bought the farm from his parents. Then the good times began for us.

Dad had known few of the comforts of life, and certainly none of the niceties, and he was determined to do better by his family than his parents had done by theirs. There was to be none of this one-banana-a-year business in his household. We had fresh fruit the year round. We had butter, not lard, on our bread. After the weather got cold he would butcher a beef and hang the carcass in the smokehouse. When we needed meat he simply went out and sliced off whatever Mother had ordered. Sometimes we had steak for breakfast.

The old house was much too small for the five of us to live in comfortably. Its windows were loose and let in the cold, and the chimneys did not draw well. But there was a simple remedy for all of this—Father built a new house.

My mother was a talented musician but had nothing to play except a secondhand organ. Dad bought her a new piano, one of the best on the market.

Christmases were joyous times with many gifts piled under the tree, which was ablaze with lighted candles. (They kept a bucket of water handy in case of fire.)

Winters were wonderful times when the ground was covered with snow so deep that we children could tunnel our way from the house to the barn. Inside the house, all was snug and warm. The kitchen always smelled delightfully with the aroma of yeast working its merry way in a glass jar of potato water that was kept at the right temperature on the warming closet of the kitchen range.

As soon as any appreciable amount of snow had fallen and it began to look like winter would hold, my father would take the wheels off the wagon and put the sled runners on. When we went to town he layered the wagon with straw, and we sat on the floor, huddled together out of the wind and covered with an old buffalo robe. Away we would go to the merry jingling of sleigh bells!

Sometimes the drifts of snow were so deep that the horses could not get through them. Then Dad would have to detour, driving the horses, huffing and snorting mightily in the frosty air, right up over the fences that were buried under drifts as hard as rock and quite capable of holding up both sleigh and passengers.

In the summer we took the surrey, but there was a limit to the number of miles you could expect work horses to take us in one day. It followed naturally, then, that we should have a car. It was the first car in the neighborhood, a clattering Model T with pancake-thin wheels, wide running boards, and black side curtains with isinglass windows that snapped on when it rained.

The salesman gave Dad a brief driving lesson when he delivered the car, taking him down the road a couple of miles while he explained the intricacies of the clutch and the brake. Dad drove back and was doing quite well until he came into the yard and the barn loomed up in front of him. He instinctively pulled back on the steering wheel and yelled, "Whoa!" But the Model T wasn't listening and he crashed into the barn.

But Dad soon got the knack of driving and the Model T opened up a whole new world for us. For the first time, we could venture fifteen or twenty miles from home and still be fairly certain to get back the same day. We went to town to shop and attend church and we visited our neighbors and went to county fairs.

Mother made all our clothing and always out of new material. A lot of women made their daughters' bloomers out of flour sacks and the girls were forced to go around with "Gold Medal" stamped on their unmentionables. But our mother didn't approve of this sort of thing. Ours were made of new sateen and they had very tight elastic around the legs and waists. They could be pulled down only with the most determined effort and, when you finally succeeded in getting them down, you could see shrively red rings around your legs where the circulation had been cut off all day.

Our bloomers were pristine white and, when Mom had them washed and hung out on the line, the breeze would catch them and they would balloon out proudly. In a way, our bloomers were status symbols, like the black velvet hat with the ostrich plume hanging down the back that my mother wore to church, and the gold bracelet that my father brought home for Mother one day when he sold a load of hogs.

Bloomers you wore underneath—everybody knew that. But one time Mother made something that looked like bloomers for my sister and me, except that these were to be worn on the outside. They were knickers, very new and very daring, and we wore them to the country fair, where they caused quite a stir. Before the day was over we felt like a couple of Hester Prynnes braving a Sunday meeting with little Pearl in her arms. One lady went so far as to call us hussies.

Hussies indeed! We were swathed from head to foot with enough cotton broadcloth to have made twenty bikinis. The middy blouses had high collars and long sleeves with cuffs that buttoned tightly around our wrists. The pants had elastic bands around the waist; they were cut enormously full and pleated into cuffs that buttoned under our knees. We wore high-topped shoes and long stockings that were clutched firmly by determined garters somewhere within the confines of our commodious bloomers. The garters, in turn, were fastened to pantywaists that slipped on over our heads.

It was a foolproof system guaranteed not to expose a square inch of forbidden flesh anywhere, providing that nothing came unhooked or unbuttoned. Of course, there was some danger that we would die from heat prostration, but that was another story. The main thing was to keep that body hidden, and hide it we did.

How simple and how beautiful were our lives in those days! There was no end to the good food. We were proudly clad. We were loved at home and accepted among our peers at church and school. There wasn't a cloud in our sky—or so my brother Don and my sister Gladys and I thought.

Then, with wrenching suddenness, it was all gone.

My father had paid more for the farm than he should have and had invested too much in fencing and tiling the low, wet ground. A short, severe depression hit the farmers in 1922, and he was faced with too many debts and could not hold on to the farm.

So, finally, the new house and the gold bracelet and the piano and the Model T had come home to roost. If Dad had only saved the money he spent for these things he probably could have weathered the storm. But he must have been skating on pretty thin financial ice for some time, because he had borrowed against his equity in the farm. There was some messy business when Grandfather had to go to court and pay fifteen hundred dollars before he could get clear title to his land again, and he was furious.

But my grandparents could have helped my father out had they chosen to do so. They had plenty of money, and the farm had been improved. It was worth more than it had been when they sold it to my father. So it wasn't purely a matter of money. They remembered how "safing" they had always been when they were young and they thought my parents should have done the same. They loved that money and they did not want to part with it. Now it loomed larger in their eyes than their oldest son.

We knew at the time that they had no pity on us and, indeed, we thought they no longer loved us. And Grandfather did take a long time to cool down. But my grandmother was devoted to that son who had caused her to make such a fast trip after the cows that day, and I think if she had known about his tears, she would have defended him and might have coaxed Grandfather into giving him another chance.

I can still remember the day when my father came home from town, after having conferred with Grandpa and the banker and had found out that all was lost. He walked wearily into the house, his broad shoulders bent, his face ravaged and unbelieving.

"Well, it's all over now," he said. "It's all gone—the farm, the livestock, everything."

The tears streamed down his face. It was the first time I had ever seen my father cry and the effect on me was traumatizing. A pall of sorrow settled over my young heart. I loved my father with a passion tantamount to adoration. His pain became my pain. At that moment I knew heartbreak. I wanted to

run to him and take him in my arms and comfort him as a
mother would her child. But I was too stunned and too stricken
to say a word.

Many years later, when my father died of a massive heart
attack that had lasted only a few minutes, I was to search myself, mull over in my mind all the things that had been left
unsaid and should not have been left unsaid, and I was to wish
that I had run to him that day and mingled my tears with his.
The sadness of that hour is still sharp in my mind. I hurt then
and I hurt now, whenever I think about it. My father's pain is
still with me — his pain at having lost everything when all he
had done was try to provide well for his family. And there is
another pain that will not go away — the pain of that young,
intelligent, studious lad who was taken out of school and sent
to do a man's work long before he was ready for it — and all for a
few paltry dollars.

And so the happy years ended. I was eight then, my
brother eleven, and my sister thirteen. We had some rough
years ahead of us.

We could not bear to watch that last day when the livestock
was being sold. It tore us apart. How could we be sure that the
horses would go to someone who would treat them well? Would
the man who bought Babe, the old mare, help her find her
stall, now that she was blind? We could not bear to listen to the
cries of the auctioneer. We shut the kitchen door and did not
even look out until it was all over.

Grandpa's new renter bought the cows. Grandfather,
magnaninous toward a stranger, had loaned him the money to
buy them. Early the next morning — our moving day — the new
man arrived to milk the cows. Years later, my mother recalled
with bitterness how he had refused us a pitcher of milk for our
breakfast.

But then he came from several miles away and he didn't
know us very well. Besides, we were already down. He could
give us another kick with impunity and he knew it.

The important thing and the idea that we had to hold onto
with all our hearts was the fact that our parents would have
given a pitcher of milk gladly and without being asked. They
might have lost everything they had but they still had their
humanity.

The worst part of all this for our parents, of course, was losing the land. The farm had been home to them for a decade and they had meant to live out their lives there. Instinctively, Dad knew that he'd never get another chance, that he'd never own a farm again—and he didn't.

Nothing is more devastating to a farmer than losing his land. He identifies with it. It gives him purpose. He finds continuity with the steady march of seasons and the planting and harvesting of crops. And there is always hope. If one year is bad, there is always the chance that the next will be better.

So a farmer schemes and works and invests his money and his strength and his know how with the idea that he will eventually succeed. Surely, he thinks, the land will not fail him. It will produce and he will profit and sometime be able to pass it along to his sons and daughters.

But, for my father, this was not to be. Like countless others before him and countless others since, merely working the land and loving the land had not been enough. The means for a good livelihood simply was not there. Everything was gone.

And we had no home.

Growing Up the Hard Way

I had a damnable childhood from the very first day we left the farm.

Dad's small amount of money was gone almost at once, but he had found a job in the small town of Westgate, Iowa, and a place for us to live a couple of miles out in the country. The house was large and beautiful, set on a hill among towering pines and spruces. The most charming thing about it was the French doors between dining and living rooms, which made the two rooms appear as one. There were windows everywhere and we could see for miles around.

It was winter now and the Model T had been drained of water and the precious tires taken off, so it was of no use temporarily. Dad had to walk to and from work. He was always gone by the time we children got up in the morning, but I watched for him to come home at night and when I saw his stocky form emerge out of the cold, blue moonlight, I would run down the road to meet him. We would walk to the house hand in hand, my heart bursting with love and pity for him.

The country schoolhouse stood right across the road from us and I can remember struggling mightily with my fractions there, but we had no books and none of the other children would lend us theirs. One day the teacher came to our house to find out what the trouble was and my mother simply told her the truth — that there was no money for books and there did not seem to be any way of getting it. After that, the teacher loaned us her books with no questions asked. That solved one problem but there were many other, more serious problems all that winter, dealing with things like the need for overshoes and long underwear and the constant battle to keep everyone fed—even to buy a spool of thread so my mother could mend our clothes or sew on some buttons.

We only lived a few months in the beautiful house at the top of the hill. Then Dad got a different job, and we were off on the first of what was to be a long series of moves. My mother was determined that none of her good furniture get scratched so she wrapped each chair and table leg in long bandages like an Egyptian mummy. This got to be a barometer of our stability, and when she started to wrap furniture legs, we knew we were going to move again.

And so we went from town to town and school to school.

We lived near Westgate and in the town of Tripoli once. We lived twice in the towns of Fredericksburg, Woodbine, and Modale. Our longest stay was in Missouri Valley, where we spent seven years.

I was a sensitive child, and every time I had to walk into a strange schoolroom and brave the stares of curious classmates and the grudging acceptance of still another stern-faced teacher, I died a little. In those days children did not readily accept new classmates. Perhaps the teachers of today are more aware of this problem and make a greater effort to integrate a strange student into a class. But I was snubbed and avoided. Eventually I thought there was no use in even trying for friendship. Small wonder that I felt like throwing up every morning Monday through Friday. (On Saturdays and Sundays my stomach was just fine.)

I realized that I had to do something to retain my sanity, so I started reading seriously and soon worked myself up to the adult section of the library, where I took out several books each week and raced home to read them through my astigmatic blur. I outread every kid in the class and learned a lot, but there seemed to be an awful lot of information that I wanted and could not find in books.

For instance, what was this strange disease that my mother referred to as "the bad disease?" I looked through several dictionaries and encyclopedias but I couldn't find it anywhere under "diseases." It seemed to be associated with sinners but I couldn't find it under "sinner," either. I pondered the bad disease at length but it remained an unfathomable riddle.

I am often appalled at the knowledge of sex that even young children have these days. But, looking back, I am equally appalled at the lack of knowledge that I grew up with. Sex was never mentioned in our home. A pregnant woman was said to be "that way" or possibly "in a family way." The latter was somewhat more descriptive but not much. A new baby didn't seem anything to be proud of until it had been born and decently swathed in innumerable layers of clothing and had had time to bleach out a little. At least, that is the way it appeared to me. Very probably the real reason a newborn was kept at home was because his mother thought fresh air might be bad for him. Colic, you know. As for sunshine—what infant needed that?

Abortion was never discussed, although I heard my mother telling my father one day about one of our female relatives who was "pretty handy with the hatpin." But I thought hatpins were something you used to pin your hat on your head with and, as the lady in question was a stylish dresser, I naturally assumed that she was pretty handy pinning her hats on her head.

My ignorance could very well have gotten me into trouble one day. I was in the fifth grade and we had just moved to the town. I went to the store on an errand for my mother and was just standing there, admiring the jewelry in a showcase, when the owner of the store walked up to me.

"You like that stuff?" he asked.

I nodded mutely, my eyes glued to a pair of seventy-nine cent earrings.

"Come into the back room with me and I'll let you have anything you want out of this showcase," he said.

Of course, I knew nothing, nothing at all. But some sixth sense seemed to tell me that I shouldn't go into the back room with that old man, and I declined politely and went about my business for my mother. So total was my ignorance that I did not even consider the incident important enough to tell my mother or my father about.

So sex, which should have been spelled SEX in my mind, didn't get emphasized at all, because you couldn't very well attach importance to something you hadn't heard about.

Entertainment was another word that deserved to be emphasized. But it wasn't, mainly because people hadn't heard about it and didn't expect to have it. There was no movie house, no library, and no swimming pool in one small town. In the winter you stayed in by the fire and maybe did a little embroidery. In the summer you sat on the porch and if the weather was hot you fanned yourself with a big, round, Japanese fan that was made of pleated paper and had a long handle on it. You took the same fan to church with you on Sunday. Cranking up the ice cream freezer was a big deal, made even more important by the fact that you didn't do it more than two or three times each summer.

One town that we lived in was so small that Main Street was only one block long. There was a drugstore, a hardware store, a filling station, a grocery store (because people had to eat) and a funeral parlor (because people had to die). There was also an aged doctor, who had a small office a half block off Main Street. He was there when somebody broke an arm or went into a coma. He wasn't too heavy on diagnosing but if you went there he would check the fuzz on your tongue. He dispensed pills off his own shelf, but he didn't have any bottles — at least, none that he wanted to give away — so he wrapped your pills in little pieces of newspaper. My father bought cream and eggs in a little building that stood on the corner. There wasn't a whole lot of *entertainment* in this town, either.

But there was some *excitement* occasionally, like when the *sheriff* drove through town and you knew he was trying to catch somebody *red-handed* at his *still*. It was also exciting when the sheriff drove back without any prisoner and you knew then that somebody had *tipped the bootlegger off.*

In some ways, that little town was reminiscent of the Old West. We had a one-armed night marshal and he saw to it that nobody got robbed and the drunks stayed off the streets. Alcoholism was not considered a disease then. It was considered a crime, and a police officer didn't have to smell anybody's breath or make him walk a straight line before he could arrest him.

One night I was awakened by loud talk and a lot of swearing and I went to the window to see what the ruckus was about. Under the glare of the corner street light, I saw a drunk staggering his way across the street and saw the one-armed marshal there, waiting for him. Suddenly, the marshal lifted his arm high and brought his night stick down over the drunk's head with a skull-shattering blow. He fell to the sidewalk and the marshal grabbed him by his collar and dragged him off to jail.

So *drunkenness* and *jail* became important words in my mind. But *police brutality* didn't, because I was only ten then and I had never heard of police brutality—only seen it. But *bootlegging* became a big word in my mind and it stayed that way practically all the time I was growing up.

Later on, during the worst of the depression years, we had a small grocery store, on the theory that people had to eat, even though the times were bad. But they weren't eating much, not even with bread at ten cents a loaf and butter at fifteen cents a pound. Most orders were less than a dollar; a three-dollar order was a rarity.

However, we did have one customer whose wife would come in the store and give us a really big order, maybe even a ten-dollar one. He was a bootlegger and he had a still out on an island in the Missouri River. For the convenience of his clientele, he kept a couple of boats tied to a tree on the Iowa side of the river, so there was no long wait in slaking one's thirst. He was reputed to have made pretty good booze. He was also careful about his customers and made sure they left the island while they were still sober enough to realize they couldn't walk on water. So nobody got drowned, and all the bootlegger had to worry about was the county sheriff and the Feds who, incidentally, never did discover his secret.

How we loved to see that bootlegger's wife come to our store! At a time when all except the rich people had to count every penny, she was able to buy anything she wanted. I was a teenager then and I envied her. I was careful to keep the pound packages of yeast she bought out of the sight of the other customers, who might see them, put two and two together and go tattling to the sheriff.

There was another bootlegger who hauled whiskey in from Canada. He prospered for many years only because he had a Studebaker so fast that nothing on the road—even the Feds—could catch up with him. They set up roadblocks and succeeded in stopping him a couple of times but they couldn't find any contraband in his car. It was a long time before they discovered that his car had a double floor and that the whiskey bottles were sandwiched in between. He had to go to jail and I thought that was a pity, for he inadvertently added a great deal of pleasure to my life. If it hadn't been for him we would never have had *The Car.* His Studebaker was confiscated and sold at auction and my father bought it for a hundred dollars. It was a sleek, long, black touring car and Dad delighted in driving it as fast as it would go. We would skim over the dusty roads with the wind blowing in from all sides and my mother would have to clutch her hat with both hands to keep it from blowing off her head. We made many trips to Evalina's house in that Studebaker and riding in it stands out yet as one of the highlights of my young life.

The Depression left its mark on everybody. People survived only by great sacrifice and heroic effort. My aunt, whose husband could not find a job, supported him and herself and her destitute brother by washing milk bottles at a dairy for ten cents an hour. A man who had a job that paid a dollar a day was considered flush with money. Well-educated men who had once had good jobs wept with joy when they started building toilets for the W.P.A.

We thought these hard times were going to last forever. The whole country seemed to be tied up in one big knot of hopelessness and despair. It was not a good time to grow up.

Because of the moving, I had no sense of belonging anywhere. So my childhood and youth had been complicated by this insecurity. I had, I realized many years later, turned out to be a hopeless neurotic. Evalina had thought her youth did not last long enough. But I thought mine lasted too long; it had, in fact, seemed interminable. Psychiatrists, whose reasoning is often as convoluted as the brains they pick, will tell you that having a worrisome childhood is not all that bad, that it may make one more determined, more ambitious, and possibly more creative. I have never believed a word of that. I had one of those damnable childhoods and I can't see that it did a thing for me.

I grew up in years, if not stability, and then I met and married William. He was tall; I was short. He was dark; I was a mousy blond. He was an extrovert; I was an introvert — none of which made a damn bit of difference to either of us. But later, when I began to have a better understanding of the differences in our personalities, I would often tell him that he would have been happier if he had married somebody else.

"You should have married Annabelle. She's more your type," I would say.

"She'd have driven me crazy," he would invariably answer.

Apparently, I didn't drive him crazy. It was a sort of a back-handed compliment but it never failed to satisfy me—at least for a few days.

William was earning fifteen dollars a week driving a truck when we were married. It wasn't much but at least he had a job. The sack in which you can easily put twenty dollars worth of groceries now could be filled for less than a dollar then, so our money did go quite far. But there was only enough for the most pressing necessities. We had no entertainment or frills of any kind. However, lots of people were in the same boat and that was all that made it bearable.

We had a baby boy, whom I named Don, after my brother. He was a bright-eyed, curly-haired youngster and I adored him. William and I were young and healthy. We could look down the road and see what our future would probably be: he would bring home the bacon and I would cook it. We would make no great waves anywhere but we would be fairly content.

Then something happened that was to change our lives almost overnight. William's brother, at thirty-three, died very suddenly of an illness that his doctor hadn't been able to diagnose. He was a farmer and had rented his first place and moved on it just that spring. Out of our shock and sorrow there arose the strong consensus within the family that William should be the one to step into his brother's shoes. William was going to be a farmer!

And I was going to be a farmer's wife.

We Take to the Hills

BUT there was some lengthy haggling before we actually decided to go to the farm. Leaving a job in town where William had a paycheck every week was not to be taken lightly. However, his family was enthusiastic about our prospects. There was no doubt in anybody's mind—all we had to do was move to the farm and we would be entering the good life. They explained to me just how good it would be. We would have no house rent to pay, and no electricity bills. We could raise a garden and have our own milk, cream, butter, eggs, and meat. In the fall we would have corn and hog money coming in and that could be used to pay off the bank or buy more machinery or livestock. I remembered how my mother had taken eggs to town to sell and how she always seemed to have plenty of grocery money. Life on the farm when I was a kid had been pretty good and maybe William and I could do as well, I told myself. The more I thought about it, the more certain I was that I wanted to go. However, William was still undecided so I did not say anything one way or another.

We had several days of uncertainty and, as usual, there was a lack of communication between William and me. William thought I didn't want to go to the farm, although I said I did. I thought he didn't want to go to the farm, although he said he did. His mother encouraged him to go, although she told him she didn't think I'd like farm life, which, when translated back from mother-in-law-ese, meant that she didn't think I'd like all that hard work. (She was right about that.) It was true. I would be giving up a life of comparative leisure for a life of hard work.

And I did not seem to have a burning desire to sacrifice myself in order to keep the horses in the family, an idea that seemed paramount in William's family. I suppose all this came through to my mother-in-law who, by the way, was an excellent woman.

Finally, William pinned me down. Did I, or didn't I, want to go to the farm? I said I thought I'd love it, because I was still thinking about all those wonderful years I had spent on the farm as a child.

So it was decided. William would quit his job in town and we would go to the farm. Our sister-in-law moved her things out of the house and we made plans to move in as soon as possible. Just *how* soon nobody said. I started packing but I didn't hurry myself. I had a baby to take care of, didn't I? And small babies took up lots of time. Surely nobody could expect me to move in less than two weeks. What I was doing, of course, was trying to stay in the house in town, with its sunny windows, electricity, hot and cold running water, and cozy bathroom as long as I could.

William must have known that he would have to prick the bubble of my procrastination sooner or later, because early one morning after he had been to the farm and done the chores, he strode into my kitchen and asked tersely, "You ready?"

"Ready for what?" I asked.

"Ready to go to the farm. We can't put this off any longer. It's time we took the bull by the horns. I've got the bays and the hayrack out back. Let's get a move on."

I went outside and looked at the hayrack. As hayracks went, I suppose it was as good as any other. But it had spaces between its boards big enough to let a small elephant slip through.

"You mean we're going to move in that thing?" I asked incredulously.

"Sure. Why not? Farmers do it all the time," he answered.

William was already moving the furniture out the back door and it did not take long to load everything we possessed into the hayrack. I made a quick tour of the house to make sure that we hadn't left anything behind. I admired the polished oak floors and the wide windows where my house plants had done so well, and I took advantage of the bathroom for the last time. I made a mistake in the bathroom. I should have kissed the stool goodby. That was the thing I was going to miss the most.

And so, finally, we were off. It was a strange caravan, the hayrack creaking under the unwieldy load, William standing up driving the horses and I, bringing up the rear in our old coupe, with four-month-old Donny, and Sandy, our feisty terrier.

I expected to see the horses run off at any moment, but I knew that William had perfect confidence in them. They were a beautiful team and William drove them proudly. Bud was a gelding, an immense animal weighing perhaps twelve hundred pounds. Beauty was a mare not much smaller than her mate. They were full brother and sister and, to the casual observer, they were almost identical, although Bud's mane was darker. Bud plodded along calmly but Beauty tossed her head nervously at every passing car.

Donny, lulled by the long ride, went to sleep. Sandy stretched himself to his full length and put his front feet on the dash, watching his beloved master with those strange animals that he did not trust. His whole body quivered with anxiety. "Relax!" I ordered. But he only laid his ears back and growled menacingly, ready to spring to William's assistance if he needed him.

The long ride gave me time to ponder what life on the farm would be like. That grand old man, F.D.R., was in the White House and he had promised that all farmers would have electricity in time. But it had not gotten out our way yet and there was no telling when it would. So I would have no washing machine, no electric iron, no vacuum sweeper. Furthermore, there was no water piped into the house. I had to admit that I would be no better off on the farm than my mother had been thirty years ago. It was a sobering thought.

Well, then, if I wouldn't have running water, or electricity, or even a good lamp to read by—what would I have? The answer that came to mind was "not much." Not unless you considered the fact a farm was a good place to raise a family, that now I would be a supportive member of the family instead of just a housewife. And William and I might become closer to each other now that we would be away from other people. These all seemed to be logical reasons that justified our going to the farm.

I knew that I wasn't going to like the house on the farm. It was a square, two-story salt box thing with windows and doors in all the wrong places. But it would be a roof over our heads, and, if Evalina could live in a log cabin and raise all those young'uns, I figured I ought to be able to live in that salt box.

It was late in the afternoon when we arrived at the farm. William maneuvered the hayrack up to the front porch and began to set the furniture in the living room. He carried in the table and chairs and set up the bed. Lastly, he built a fire in the kitchen range.

That done, he pulled on his cap and said, "Cobs for the stove are out in the shed. Wood is stacked behind the shed. The water hydrant is down at the bottom of the hill. Don't forget to gather the eggs."

I looked around at the rolled-up rugs and the furniture in the middle of the floor and the boxes of stuff piled around wherever there was a place for them and I said, "Can't you help me with some of this work?"

"Can't help you with anything right now. It's time to do the chores. Besides, Beauty has a bad limp and I think she may have a rock in her foot. I'll have to dig that out. She has to be taken care of first," he answered.

So that's how it's going to be, I thought grimly. You've got to carry the water and the wood and the cobs and gather the eggs. What's more you're playing second fiddle to a twelve-hundred-pound horse. Realization was dawning fast. I felt like a high class embezzler who had just been snatched from his penthouse and sentenced to twenty years on the rock pile. This work was going to take a bit of getting used to. Maybe William's mother had been right about me. Maybe I wasn't the type to be a farmer's wife at all.

But our rural Rubicon had been crossed, and it was too late to turn back now. It was a good thing I did not know what lay ahead—or I would have turned tail and run.

Our future held some appalling statistics: seven pails of water per day for the next eighteen years came to an approximate total of three hundred and forty-five tons of water pumped and carried into the house for cooking and dishwashing alone, excluding the water brought in for laundry and bathing purposes; six trips each day to the ugly two-holer out back totaled up to thirty-nine thousand, four hundred and twenty trips in eighteen years.

But these statistics were blessedly unrevealed and lay in our future—to be endured a bucket and a trip at a time, in winter's cold and summer's heat, with as much fortitude as we could muster.

The hens had done themselves proud that day and when I gathered the eggs I found seventy-six big, beautiful brown ones, all much larger and fresher than anything we could buy in a store. All for nothing, too, I thought to myself—not being smart enough yet to consider all the grain and commercial feed and oyster shell they had eaten. That realization would come later. For now, I was just as pleased with my hens as their lord and master, the red rooster who surveyed his harem proudly from the top-most perch of the henhouse.

It was getting dark when I heard William coming up from the barn, the metal milk pails making pleasant tinkling sounds when they rubbed against his overalls. He brought two steaming pails of milk into the kitchen and poured them into the separator, a machine with a large bowl and two spouts that sat in the corner of the room. Soon he had cream coming out of one spout and skim milk out the other. The skimmed milk would be used to feed the pigs, he said.

We ate supper that night by the dim light of a kerosene lamp while William told me about Beauty. She really did have a rock in her foot, he said, but she had stood patiently while he held up her foot and dug it out.

"I'll have to take the skimmed milk down to the sows," William said when he had finished eating. "And I may not be back for awhile because it looks like the old black cow is going to calve and I'd better stay there until I'm sure everything is all right."

I wiped fresh-from-the-henhouse egg from the baby's face and said, "I'm going to put Donny to bed now and I may even go to bed myself. I can't see to work in this lamplight. Anyway, it's been a long day and I'm tired."

"Go to bed if you want to," William answered. "I don't know what time I'll be back. It depends on the cow."

I was asleep when William came up from the barn, but he woke me up to tell me the good news.

"The black cow had a calf, a nice big, bull calf. And I didn't have to do a thing to help her," he exulted.

"Well, bully for her," I said, and went back to sleep.

So we had taken to the hills for good now. We had two hundred acres of land which, if by some miracle it could have been flattened out, would have been four hundred acres. We owned, in conjunction with the bank, eight cows, one brand new bull calf, ten brood sows ready to "pig," a hundred laying hens, and four horses—or perhaps they owned us. Because all our waking hours were going to be devoted one way or another to the care of those creatures. If there was ever any question of priorities, you knew instinctively which ones were going to win out—and it would not be the people who lived in the salt box at the top of the hill.

Life in the Salt Box

THE barn had been built with an eye to the convenience of the man who worked in it and the comfort of the creatures who inhabited it, but the house had been built with one purpose in mind—to put a roof over one's head. No fuss, no feathers. Just a roof over one's head.

And this made sense, too. You had to keep the animals comfortable because you made money off them and if they were miserable they didn't have big enough litters or produce as much milk or do whatever it was they were supposed to do to bring in the money.

But with a house it was different. Nobody ever made a dime off a house, and apparently nobody cared if a woman ran her legs off or ruptured herself while she was trying to do her work. It was livestock that counted—not women.

The house on the hill must have been fifty years old when we moved into it and it made me think of a middle-aged woman. Its joints were creaking, its walls were wrinkling and its pendulous porches were sagging. It was hard to imagine the house as ever having been beautiful, even in the first blush of youth.

No matter how bright the day, not one ray of sunshine ever got into the living, dining room, or kitchen. The living room had one east window but some misguided soul had seen fit to hang a porch roof over it. There were three north windows in the house but the only thing we could see through them was the top of a car as it passed down the road. Not the whole car. Just the top.

The rooms were square, or nearly so, and there wasn't a room in the house with any individuality. The downstairs bedroom was so small that by the time you got the bed wedged in, there was scarcely enough room for a dresser. Just pulling out a drawer could be a shin-bruising experience.

Furthermore, the house was in reverse. Everybody came in through the kitchen door. Nobody ever came in at the living room door because it was on the wrong side of the house. The living room should have been where the kitchen was and then callers would not have had to be ushered past the cream separator and the dirty dishes and the cob baskets.

But no matter. That was the way the house was and no amount of complaining was going to change things. Besides, the forty-three parts of the cream separator were supposed to be washed and covered with a white cloth when not in use, the dishes were supposed to be done and out of sight at all times, and the cob baskets were supposed to be hidden behind the stove.

The kitchen was where I spent most of my time. This was where I cooked, washed milk pails, did the laundry and the ironing, the baby tending, and the mailman watching. Here we ate and here we took baths. The kitchen was a multi-purpose room. It was seldom unoccupied and seldom orderly.

In the west corner of the kitchen a tired sink squatted over a rusty drain pipe. There was a small shelf between the sink and the corner and here sat a red pitcher pump. Its purpose was to bring rain water up from a cistern under the porch, the rain water, in turn, having drained off the roof of the house. A sloping kitchen floor had allowed the drain pipe to slope and because the drain pipe sloped the sink sloped and because the sink sloped the pitcher pump sloped. It was sad. On the east wall of the kitchen there was a large cupboard which was supposed to hold everything—dishes, pans, groceries, and anything else you wanted to hide.

The focal point of the kitchen was the big, black cookstove which had probably been manufactured before the turn of the century. When it was new it must have been the pride and joy of its first owner, and it still had a nice, slate blue finish when it was polished up. It had a round knob like a belly button in the middle of the oven door and there was lots of fancy, nickel-plated scrollwork around the outside of the oven door and around the warming closets at the top.

The oven was large enough to bake six loaves of bread at one time and on the end of the stove was a reservoir that held ten gallons of water if you had the ambition to keep it filled. The stove had no legs, but that was the way all the old ranges were. They sat flat on the floor and, because they were sometimes used for forty or fifty years, they rusted out underneath before anybody knew about it. You found out when the house caught on fire.

"Devil," as I was soon calling him, ingested, digested, and eliminated. Most of my day was taken up carrying cobs or wood, shoving the fuel into his belly, and taking out the resulting ashes. He required two or three baskets of cobs plus several armloads of wood each day. Digestion was facilitated by jabbing him in his gut with an iron poker. You had to be careful to turn his damper just right. If you left it too far open you soon found that all the heat had gone up the chimney and you had carried all that fuel for nothing. If you shut the damper too tightly Devil choked up and spewed foul-smelling gas out around his lids.

Devil and I carried on a continuing feud. He seemed to be a living thing, his sole purpose in life to thwart my will. He never got hot until long after I myself had reached the boiling point. At such times I would stand back and give him a good swift kick right in his nickel-plated belly button and yell, "Get hot, damn you! Get hot!"

I used to swear that I had never seen any more exasperating inanimate object in my life. I loathed the work he required and the dirt he made. But he also had a lot of admirable qualities, many of which I did not appreciate until much later.

He had a large cooking space at different temperatures and I could fry, boil, stew, and simmer all at the same time. If I set a pan of curdled milk on the back of the range when there was almost no fire in it I could come up with some elegant cottage cheese. By taking long cobs, the ends of which had been lightly dipped in kerosene, I could get a flame that was just right for angelfood cakes. I have not been able to duplicate the lightness and fluffiness of these cakes in an electric range to this day. And these were not the box mixes. They were the kind made from scratch, with hand-whipped egg whites.

I don't think cake mixes were on the market in those days and we farm women probably wouldn't have used them if they had been. We already had everything we needed to cook with. The eggs, butter, milk, and cream were there for the taking—not free, of course, but not to be paid for in cash, either. We tended to use them lavishly. Novice that I was those first few months, I soon learned to use everything the farm provided.

Gravy was always made with milk. There were plenty of eggs and milk for pies and custard. Our cream was thick and yellow and a few minutes beating was all it took to get a bowlful of whipped cream that was wonderful on desserts. Sour milk made exceptionally tender pancakes. I could make a rich chocolate cake by using sour cream and cocoa. The ten or twelve eggs used in making an angelfood cake scarcely made a dent in the number the hens would lay in one day.

None of this would have been possible without Devil, of course. When I learned how to manage him, how to combine green wood with dry to get a longer lasting fire, how to set his damper, and just where to cook what on his commodious surface—then I had better luck with him. I was never fond of him, but I recognized his versatility. He kept us unmercifully hot in the summer, but he kept us comfortably warm in the winter, and for this we were grateful. For sheer utility he had every modern gas or electric range backed clear off the map. There have been many times when I've had to cook for a large crowd of people and wished I had him back, ugly and dirty and crotchety though he was.

We got much pleasure from the butter, cream, milk, and eggs in those first months. Later on, we would butcher a hog, William assured me. All of these things were evidence that we were entering that good life we had hoped we would find when we went to the farm.

Certainly William seemed happy. Seeing the livestock and crops growing gave him a lot of satisfaction and he worked long hours without complaint. But he was a man doing one man's work, and I was a woman doing three women's work—or thought I was. We could have bought a different washing machine with a gasoline engine on it. But we thought electricity was just around the corner and a gasoline engine would have

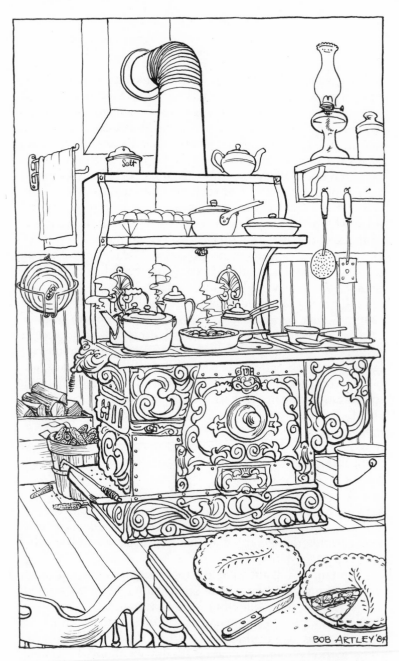

None of this would have been possible without Devil

meant washing on the porch, even in the winter. I preferred to do it in the kitchen.

William carried all the water for the laundry. But it was I who performed the drudgery of washing on the "board." The washboard was made of corrugated glass, set in a wooden frame with six-inch legs. I set it down in a tub of hot water, laid a piece of clothing across it, rubbed the spots with cake soap, and got right to work, my torso going up and down like a pump handle. Piece by piece I soaped, scrubbed, lifted, dunked, and sloshed the bedding, shirts, dresses, towels, and underwear. Sheets and overalls were an abomination and could not be properly done no matter how hard I tried. (Diapers and baby clothes I did separately and on different days.) After the wash had been taken through a sudsing and two rinse waters I wrung it out and hung it outdoors to dry. This process took almost all day, even in the summer, because I could never get much of the water out. I came through washdays with red, swollen hands, an aching back, and the disposition of a dyspeptic tiger.

Yet the crowning touch came when I ironed with the sad irons. These little devils have been aptly named, for they are surely the saddest invention ever to be foisted off on woman-kind. They were boat shaped, about two thirds the size of an electric iron, and had one detachable handle which served all three irons. You had to change irons often to be sure they were hot enough and they often had soot on the bottoms so you had to wipe them off first. Devil had to be kept at his hottest for as long as it took to do the ironing.

Needless to say I have no patience with antique lovers who become ecstatic at the sight of a wash boiler, a washboard, or a sad iron. Nothing fills me with any greater loathing.

There was one relic of those days that I wish I had kept, however. This was a wall lamp with a shiny reflector behind it that we used in the kitchen. I do not remember now what I did with it. I must have thrown it away with other memorabilia from those years, for I was young and thoughtless then and could not foresee a time when it could be of any value to me. But I believe I could look at it now without pain.

To do the work on the farm under these conditions you had to have the strength of a Percheron, the speed of a gazelle, and the patience of a saint, all very fine attributes which I seemed to have in short supply. Just like the Jill in the nursery rhyme, I was forever going down the hill to fetch a pail of water. With a bucket in each hand I was carrying approximately thirty pounds of water and I arrived at the house with my back bent and my arms stretched out like a female gorilla that spent her days swinging from the trees. But carrying two pails of water at once helped to equalize the strain on my shoulder sockets.

Besides, when I carried two pails at once I was, in effect, killing two birds with one stone. I discovered very soon after coming to the farm that this was the only way to go. Even at that, there always seemed to be a multiplicity of birds and a paucity of stones. You had to combine tasks because more birds kept flying out of the bushes all the time.

There were only two houses in our neighborhood that had water piped into the kitchen sinks. Nobody had a bathroom. The same galvanized tub that we used to wash clothes in served as a bath tub, into which only a small, bendable portion of one's anatomy would fit. So the best way to take a bath was to stand up in the tub and sponge off.

Every farm had its two-or-three hole Necessary, as the Victorians used to call it, sitting conspicuously out in the back yard somewhere. High on each side of the Necessary was a hole cut out in the shape of a half moon or a diamond. There were more half moons than diamonds, and if you had taken a poll the half moons would have won hands down. These half moons added a sort of aesthetic touch and through them you could look up and see a small slice of sky in the daytime and a few stars at night. It helped take your mind off where you were sitting, which was cold, possibly with snow on the seat in the winter, and hot, possibly with spiders under the seat in the summer.

Sometimes we used a chamber pot at night. This was a heavy porcelain vessel that is now considered quite a find in an antique shop, although I am sure I don't know why anybody would want one. My mother had an earthy name for the chamber pot, no doubt an appellation that had been passed down from Evalina. Mother called it the "thundermug," which added a touch of humor to this unlovely but necessary adjunct to a household.

The thundermug was just dandy if you had it in the closet when you needed it at night. But I, being somewhat absent-minded in these respects, would often forget to bring it back to the house after I had emptied it in the mornings. So if one had to go out in the middle of the night to retrieve it, one might as well attend to the calls of nature in the Necessary and be done with it.

One developed one's own rules with respect to the Necessary. One rule was never to go within a hundred feet of it without taking advantage of its propinquity, for if you did you would just have to seek it out thirty minutes later anyway.

Another thing you could do was train yourself to wait. This was helpful in avoiding nighttime trips to the Necessary. When I awoke in misery I would simply put my mind on something else, like buying new furniture, or new clothes, or taking a trip to Europe—all impossible dreams at the moment.

But this ploy did not work all the time, either, for I found that after I had driven to Chicago by car, sailed through the St. Lawrence Seaway, and crossed the Atlantic Ocean, I was too uncomfortable to keep my mind on Buckingham Palace when I finally got there. After a night like this my memory would miraculously improve and I might not forget the thundermug for a week or more.

All of this seems humorous only in retrospect—the water carrying, that old black Devil, the Necessary, the cob and wood carrying, the battles to eradicate the mice in the old houses we moved into. None of it seemed humorous at the time. It was all very exasperating then. I put up with it only because there wasn't anything else to do. William caught the full blast of my disgruntlement, of course, but I seldom said anything about it to the other women, who were, after all, doing the same kinds of work that I was.

Happily there was one day each month when we got away from it all. That was when the neighborhood club met. I always enjoyed these meetings. They were the only times we could relax and enjoy ourselves and forget the burdensome work awaiting us at home. Entertaining the club women was a lot of work, but the payoff came eleven times a year when you got to go to somebody else's house for the afternoon.

Your own club day was a very important day, a time when your reputation as a housewife, hostess, and cook was on the line. Everything in the house had to be spotless. The last vestige of dust had to be wiped away, the floors perfectly clean, the curtains freshly washed and precisely hung. You weren't supposed to have a hint of clutter anywhere.

This was just fine if you were a good housekeeper at all times. But I wasn't, and I had to begin two or three weeks in advance to get the house in shape. Even then I used to have some serious last minute crises when, in desperation, I merely opened drawers and shoved a lot of things out of sight. I never managed to be a calm and collected hostess and I still have nightmares in which I am caught with unmade beds and a mop pail sitting in the middle of the floor at the very moment when the ladies are approaching my door.

Within a radius of two or three miles from us there sat thirteen farm homes, each as isolated as a frog in his own private puddle. This area formed the immediate periphery of our world. Here lived the men with whom your husband would put up hay and the women from whom you might borrow a cup of sugar. But I seldom saw any of these people. Long days went by during which I saw no one but William, who was lucky if he had an hour to himself in the evenings and who went to sleep in his chair when he did. I would have liked to jump into the car and drive over to see some of my neighbors, but I sensed early on that this was not the thing to do. Farm women were too busy to be bothered with casual visitors, and the inference was that if you had time for this sort of thing you were probably neglecting your house, or your chickens, or your garden. And God forbid that you should neglect your house or your chickens or your garden!

There seemed to be a strict, no-nonsense code of female conduct. It was never openly elucidated, simply conveyed by a tone of voice or a seemingly harmless remark that, after you had had time to think about it, carried the sting of a scorpion. After several fruitless attempts to strike up a close, woman-to-woman relationship that first year, I finally gave up.

I missed my neighbors in town, women who "dropped in" on me at any hour of the day and who welcomed my visits in return. But everything was different now. I was a farmer's wife and I was supposed to stay home and act like one. And if I did all the things I was supposed to do I had no time to do the things I wanted to do. It was like a catch-22 situation from which there was no escape for me unless we left the farm and went back to town. That choice would have branded us as quitters and would have hurt William a great deal. So the only thing I could do was hang in there and hope that things would get better.

This led to a conclusion in which there was much truth but little comfort: life was one hell of a lot of work!

Life in the Barn

I detested the house but I loved the barn, where little things like dust and cobwebs did not matter and where every creature responded to my entry with a show of curiosity and what appeared to be genuine welcome at times. I seldom made a trip to the barn during the day unless it was to get cobs for Devil. After William came in from the field at the end of the day, however, I would put supper on hold in the warming closet and carry Donny to the barn and we would sit on the hay while William chored.

Whoever had designed the barn had been a veritable Noah. He had wisely planned a place for each breed of animal and had managed to create an atmosphere of spaciousness without sacrificing coziness. Yet he had arranged it all so the caretaker could do his work with ease and efficiency.

There were two doors on both ends of the barn and one on the side so that a breeze could blow through in the summer. I couldn't help contrasting this arrangement with the one in the hot and stuffy house, and it only served to reinforce my contention that it was livestock — not people — that counted on a farm.

A large haymow formed the focal point of the barn. In a U-shape around it were the horse stalls, the hog pens, the calf pen, and the milking "parlor." A man could begin at one end of the "U" and walk around to feed the livestock without ever having to retrace his steps or get into the pens with the animals.

William always fed the horses first. On working days each horse got several ears of corn twice a day, plus a large forkful of hay. They would take a whole ear of corn into their mouths at once, wallowing it around until they had almost every kernel off before they dropped the cob back into the feedbox. They never touched the hay until after all the corn was eaten.

These long cobs made good fuel for Devil if you waited until the horse saliva on them had dried. I could not bring myself to take the wet cobs out of the feedboxes, however, so William picked them out and tossed them into a little pile for me to get later.

The sows were fed next. Each farrowed eight or nine pigs soon after we came to the farm and their pens were alive with peppy little porkers. The sows were especially hungry now that they were nursing their babies. It always amused me to see how they flopped down for the convenience of their little ones when it came time to eat. The mothers would lie on their sides and twist their bellies up, thrusting their pink teats out invitingly while urging the piglets on with loud grunts of maternal welcome. It was almost as if they were saying, "Soup's on, kids! Come and get it!"

The little pigs were adorable. Bright, buttony eyes peeked out from under floppy ears. Pink skin showed through their baby bristles. Yet if you touched one you found that he was not bristly at all. He was as soft and smooth as silk.

But touching a baby pig was something that one did not do very often. William would sometimes hold a little one up for Donny and me to caress, but if this disturbed the sow, as it often did, he quickly put the pig back in its pen.

No other animal displays as much love for her offspring as does the sow, who has been known to fight a grizzly bear in defense of her young. Any threat is met with terrible ferocity, her jaws opened wide, her sharp teeth capable of mangling a human hand or arm in one bite. Two of our sows were downright vicious and these, of course, William left strictly alone.

The sows were always alert to danger and suspicious of any human with whom they were not familiar. However, they had no objection if you stood quietly at a respectful distance and merely admired their babies. And what mother wouldn't be proud of a brood of plump piglets lying side by side like a row of sausages?

In the evenings the barn was vibrant with the happy sounds of hay being munched, of satisfied grunts as the sows took to their beds on clean straw, and the soft squishing of milk into a pail. The cat would be sitting in her usual place, waiting for that magic moment when William would shoot a stream of milk her way.

The cows would be eating their ground corn, waiting patiently for the touch of human hands. Most of the cows stood contentedly while they were being milked, but a few of them were tail switchers and one was a kicker. She had to be immobilized by a chain from one hind leg to the other so she couldn't get either foot off the floor high enough to land a blow.

William always said that milking wasn't work and that he could rest while he did it, although I never could see how a man could get much rest sitting on a one-legged milk stool. But he made it look easy. He grasped a teat in each hand and gave a couple of warning yanks to let the cow know it was time to let down. Then the milk would begin to run and he would settle into a steady, rhythmic pulling and squeezing motion until the cow was dry. The richest milk came at the last, so if you sold cream, as we did, you had to be careful to get it all. Anyway, a cow that was not thoroughly milked out every time soon dried up.

I could never learn to milk a cow, although I tried many times. William saw my ineptitude and forbade me ever to touch a cow again, lest my awkward fumblings dry her up.

It wasn't that I needed to help with the milking chores. It was just that I thought it would be a good thing to know. I surmised that I was the only woman in the neighborhood who didn't know how to milk a cow and I was rather ashamed of that. However, it looked like I was going to have to live with my shame because I was never going to get the hang of it.

"I'd like to know why it is that I can't learn to do that," I said one evening, as William was milking away furiously.

"Do what?" William asked.

"Learn to milk."

"You can't. You're too old."

"Too old? At twenty-six?"

"Sure. People have to learn to milk when they're young."

"How young?

"Six. Eight. Ten."

"I'll never make it," I said solemnly.

Life in the barn

Each cow knew her own place among the stalls. If one cow usurped another's stall, the dispossessed one simply waited until the offender had been bopped on the flanks a few times and forced to move on.

One of the cows was a small, tawny animal of Jersey lineage. She had a flattened, almost bashed-in place in the middle of her head and she looked like a moose. She surprised us that first spring by giving birth to a red calf. So there must have been a roan or a Shorthorn bull in her recent past.

Each of the cows had a personality of her own and we quickly discerned this. Big Red was greedy and particularly bad about getting into the wrong stall. She may have done this with malice aforethought because while she was in her neighbor's place she had a chance to gobble up some of her food, and when she got back to her own stall she still had a full meal waiting. Moose-face was invariably polite and never shoved any other cow out of the way when it came time to enter the barn. The old black cow was bossy and used her horns to clear a path for herself. The horses soon learned not to kick the red and white spotted cow because she whaled away and kicked them right back. A cow was seldom just a cow. She was assertive or shy, mischievous or downright ornery—but seldom just a cow.

William put the new red calf in the pen with the black one. Now he had two to be fed twice a day by the bucket method. Calves born to milk cows are not allowed to nurse their mothers, so they must be taught to drink milk. The calves would stick their noses down into the pail and pull them out again, deciding they wanted no part of this disgusting and unnatural business. They would back off a few feet, then dash back and butt the pail like it was a living udder. It was a rare day when neither one of them spilled his milk. But all was forgiven when they finally learned to drink and had their fill and were racing around the calf pen with tails flying in the exuberance of youth.

Cats often wander from farm to farm and sometimes you think you have a cat when you don't. It was this way with our cat, who came and went as she pleased and was so standoffish that I never did succeed in making friends with her. At night she could act like a blatant hussy; by day she was aloof and haughty. And she stuck to her principles, too. There was none of this insipid brushing up against people's legs—none of this insecure meowing for food and attention. She preferred to get her own food.

I often watched Cat on the hunt in the barn. First she sniffed at the mouse hole. If it smelled promising she lay down on her stomach in front of it, not a muscle moving, her green eyes glued to the spot where the mouse might exit. Long minutes would go by but she never lost patience. Then her keen ears would detect the sound of movement in the hole. Her muscles tensed and her tail began to wave in anticipation. Soon the tiny mouse head appeared, the whiskers twitching, the beady eyes darting warily from side to side. Cat, tail and all, froze as unmoving as a post. The mouse gained confidence and very cautiously he emerged from the hole. Cat would let him get out in the open for a couple of inches and then like a flash pounced on him. There was a small squeak of surprise and pain, and then it was over. Cat did not like to eat in front of people so she carried her meal off to a place of seclusion, usually under the corncrib.

Cat was there, off and on, for a number of years. We never bothered to name her. She was just "Cat" to us. But I don't think it would have made any difference if we had given her a name. She wouldn't come when she was called, anyway. No matter how many times I called, no matter how syrupy I made my voice, she wouldn't come. She never took a bite of food from us. The only thing she would deign to do was come to the barn twice each day when the milking was being done and wait for that glorious moment when William would shoot that stream of warm milk her way.

Even so, I always admired Cat. True, she disdained the outstretched human hand, but she had survived quite handily by herself for a long time, and if she preferred a peopleless life in the haymow—who were we to say she hadn't made the better choice?

Our terrier, Sandy, was a one man dog and his master had to be protected at all costs. So each morning he left his bed behind the range and went with William to do the chores. But he never did learn to enjoy the barn, and couldn't go there without having a nervous tizzy. Cat was a creature he could take or leave, chase or ignore. But he couldn't accept those other monstrous quadrupeds. They were a real threat to him. And the noises! There was so much whinnying, so much squealing, so much bellowing. Sandy started shaking as soon as he entered the barn and never quit shaking until he was on his way back to the house.

When we first moved to the farm I was terrified by the coyotes, who began their eerie howling with the coming of darkness and kept it up all night long. The hills seemed to be full of them. By listening carefully you could trace the pack as it skulked through the timber or ran along the bottom of a ravine to come out eventually in what you knew to be an open field.

Sometimes a lone coyote would dare to come into an open field in the daylight. But he was always very cautious, moved across the field quickly, and kept himself low to the ground. He would be so furtive in his passage and would appear and disappear so quickly that you sometimes wondered if you had seen a coyote at all, or whether your eyes had played tricks on you.

However, it was at night when the coyotes really came into their own. By listening to their separate voices you could tell there were usually five or six in a pack. They started out with sharp, staccato yippings that rose in pitch to a high, steady wail like a siren, then slowly decreased in intensity to a low menacing howl. Naturally, it was too much to expect them to be synchronized. While some were yapping in a low tone, others were yipping in a high tone and others were dropping their voices for the finale.

At night I would lie awake and listen to the coyotes as they wound their way out of the timber south of the house and came closer and closer to the farm buildings. I wondered what they were after. A chicken? A little pig? I wondered if they would attack a small boy if they caught him alone and unprotected during the day?

William said that my fears were unfounded, that the coyotes were cowardly creatures who would run at the sight of a human—even a frightened female on a midnight Mecca to the Necessary. But I wasn't so sure of that, and what happened to Sandy reinforced my fears. He was a fighter, the veteran of many battles. He had courage and he knew how to fight. And it was precisely those admirable qualities, plus the urge to mate, that almost cost him his life that first spring.

Usually, when Sandy was let out in the evenings he would come back before dark, scratch at the door for admittance, and come in wagging his stubby tail in appreciation at being welcomed back to the family circle. Upon this one occasion, however, he did not return. We called repeatedly but no small, white form emerged out of the darkness. We sat up later than usual that night, wondering uneasily what had made him stay away. At midnight we decided there was no need to sit up any longer or do any more calling. I listened to the coyotes long after we had gone to bed and I thought their voices sounded especially strident and ferocious that night.

Morning came and there was still no sign of Sandy. Then, as we sat at the breakfast table, we heard him scratching and whining at the kitchen door. This was not his usual, imperious demand for admittance. This was a call for help.

We were aghast at his appearance when we let him in. One

ear was slit to ribbons and his right shoulder was a mass of cuts. He was covered with blood and scarcely able to walk. We put an old rug behind the stove and he sank miserably down upon it. Now we could see the full extent of his injuries. In addition to all his other wounds, he had been slashed the full length of his underbelly.

We could not see how he could possibly live. For several days he refused all food and drank only a little water. He bestirred himself only with great pain. We caressed him, if we could find a place that didn't hurt, and we urged him to fight his way through this battle, too.

One day he managed to get up on his forepaws and drink, and then we began to take heart. But it was two weeks before he was able to stand on all four feet and limp outdoors. He could walk only a few inches at a time and with each step his hindquarters swung to one side, so we knew he had had a serious injury to his spine.

We could only theorize about what had happened to him, of course, but we were fairly sure he had tried to join a coyote pack during the time when they were sexually active. Never having seen coyotes before, he wouldn't have recognized those dog-like creatures as enemies and had probably tried to mate with one of the females. No doubt the whole pack had attacked him at once. He, being the feisty little terrier that he was, had tried to battle it out and narrowly escaped with his life.

Sandy had never lost a fight before, nor had he known fear. But he knew fear now. He no longer barked when he heard the coyotes at night, even when he was safe in the house and he knew William was there to protect him. All he did was growl cautiously, deep down in his throat, and he was careful not to let the growl get too loud.

I had felt sorry for Sandy even before he had his fight with the coyotes. He was lonely. He had never been separated from William before but he had to be separated now. There was no way he could follow that plow or that cultivator all day long. All he could do was stay home by himself. He simply didn't belong on a farm.

And, although I was careful not to express it in so many words—and was, in fact, even ashamed to admit it to myself—I was beginning to think that he wasn't the only one.

Making Hay the Hard Way

PUTTING up hay is never an easy job, even with modern balers and choppers. But when we moved to the farm it was an especially difficult task for it was all done by hand. Five or six men collaborated in haying, helping each other until the alfalfa was safely in the barn.

You knew, of course, who the members of your hay crew would be, for they were always your closest neighbors. However, there was a well-defined protocol and you didn't even so much as cut one swath until you had first gone to your neighbors and found out if your plans would conflict with theirs. Almost always these arrangements were made amicably. It did not pay to be uncooperative with other members of your haying crew. They were the people on whom you depended most heavily. They were used to working together and they knew how you wanted the job done, so you wanted them to come willingly when you needed them. You might have trouble getting along with a man in your threshing ring but he was needed only once a year and, if you found your differences with him to be insurmountable, you could simply hire a man to take his place. But quarrel with your haying neighbor? Never! That was unthinkable.

Although it was never stated in so many words, there was a fairly strict division of labor among the men. The younger ones walked in the fields and pitched the hay onto the racks. An older man was usually asked to bring a team and rack. He had to spread the hay around when it was pitched up to him, but he didn't have to walk. Another man would be asked to drive a team on the hayfork. The farmer whose hay was being put up took the hardest and dirtiest job of all. He stayed in the barn and stacked the hay as it fell from the big fork in the ceiling. On a hot day work in the barn would become almost unbearable, and he would be soaked with sweat and his clothing plastered with dust and bits of hay when the job was done.

Although there was a division of labor among the men, there was no division of labor for a woman. You were expected to cook and serve a big meal all by yourself. Not only that, but you were expected to have the house in good order and a supply of warm water, soap, and towels ready for the men when they came in; because your husband was very busy and couldn't possibly take time to carry water and wood and cobs, you had to do all these things by yourself. And — this was the real biggie — you were supposed to have dinner ready on time.

I had heard the other women talk about cooking for hay men and threshers and, no doubt, without intending to do it, they left me with the impression that it was a big deal — a very big deal, in fact. So I was already uptight about the cooking even before I had to do it, and I didn't know whether I could do it or not.

I was soon to find out, for William strode into the kitchen one afternoon and informed me that I would be having hay men for dinner the next day.

"Hay men? Me?" I asked in alarm.

"Sure. They work here, they eat here. All the other women have to do it. Now it's your turn," he answered.

I asked him what I ought to cook but he could offer no suggestions until after I said, "Well, maybe I'll just fix a big kettle of mush."

Then he told me what the other women fixed: meat, potatoes, gravy, a couple of vegetables or a salad, and cake or pie. "Make sure there's plenty of everything," he finished.

I realized at once that my reputation was at stake. I was a town woman, strange to the ways of farm cookery and therefore I was of a different breed. No doubt the men were already wondering what kind of a meal they would get. For all they knew I might not even be able to boil water, let alone fix a big dinner for several hungry men.

We were both up at daylight the next morning, I feeling

like Marie Antoinette must have felt on her way to the guillotine. William hurried through the chores and went to town to buy the meat and other groceries I needed. We had no means of refrigeration so nothing perishable could be bought beforehand. I carried enough water and wood to last for the next seven hours and then started in on the pies. By the time Donny awoke the roast was in the oven and the potatoes were peeled and soaking in a pan of cold water. By ten o'clock the dishes and separator had been washed and the house was looking reasonably good. And I was utterly and completely pooped.

But there was no time to lose, for Devil had to be fed. He had already filled his ash pan once and I hastily took it out and emptied it so he could get his breath from down below. I kept forking the roast but it wasn't getting tender very fast and I concluded the fire wasn't hot enough. I threw some cobs in, backed up, kicked Devil square in his nickel-plated belly button and yelled, "Get hot, damn you! Get hot!"

This outburst, as usual, seemed to do both of us good. It helped me get my frustrations out and Devil began to cooperate immediately. Soon the aroma of browning beef permeated the kitchen and, when I set the potatoes on to boil, the kettle was hot within minutes.

I gave dinner everything I had that day, but it still was not ready for the table when the men came in. No doubt William had expected something like this. My tardiness was inexcusable and he was visibly embarrassed. I apologized to the men for being late with their meal.

"That's all right. The horses need a rest, anyway," Bob Irving said. "This is the first time I've worked my mare since she had her colt."

Mentally thanking the mare who had just had the colt, I redoubled my efforts and my speed in the kitchen. I suppose it was because I was in such a hurry that I didn't mash the potatoes, merely drained the water off them and poured them into a bowl whole. This thoughtless act, as it turned out, was a mistake of great magnitude.

But finally dinner was ready and the men sat down to eat. A farm wife does not sit down and eat with the men, at least we didn't in those days. There were several reasons for this, one of them being the undefined but nonetheless obligatory perception that it just wasn't done, another being that the presence of a woman was inhibiting and kept the men from talking man talk, another being that a woman had so much to do she didn't have time to sit down anyway.

I made quick observations about the men — most of whom I hadn't met before — while I scurried back and forth from the kitchen to dining room bringing in more bread, filling up the gravy bowl, pouring more coffee, and serving the pie.

Brick Nelson was well over six feet tall and had a big nose and red hair. He hadn't bothered to shave for several days and a golden beard covered his face and chin. Pete Neuman was about forty. He had a square jaw and large teeth but he was still a good-looking man. Bob Irving was about thirty, small and wiry, wearing glasses. Chris Bagley was the oldest of the crew. He was at least sixty, reed thin, with a long, sharp nose under deep-set eyes. He had a peculiar laugh that came out as a mirthless monotone, with no inflection at all, simply a haw-haw-haw.

These were our neighbors, the men who would mean the most to us, men upon whom William would have to call if there was work to be done that he couldn't handle alone, men whom we would have to depend on if we had trouble of some kind. And they would come if we needed them, the same way William would go to them if they needed him. We had lived in the neighborhood only a few weeks but already there was a bond between us, and some of these men would be helping us put up our hay for the next eighteen years.

Women are generally conceded to be the more talkative sex, but I do not agree with that idea. I can still remember how surprised I was to hear those men chatter away that day. They were obviously enjoying themselves, as happy as schoolkids skipping class for a picnic. And this was understandable, for they had to do almost all the work on their own farms alone, and had to spend long days in the field where there was no one to talk to. They had companionship now, and they made the most of it.

Everything is different now, of course. Almost no one puts loose hay in the barn. It is all chopped or baled and a farmer does almost all the work by himself. The old, close-knit, congenial crew of five or six hay men is almost a thing of the past. In some ways, this is a pity.

Not that neighborliness is dead—far from it. Let some calamity befall a farmer, perhaps at a time of year when he has corn that needs picking, and other farmers for miles around will converge with tractors and wagons and picker-shellers and in a matter of hours his crop will be binned or cribbed. Not only that, but the women will bring food and prepare and serve a dinner to the men.

I cooked many meals for hay men and threshers in my role as a farmer's wife, but the memory of most of them is blurry, I suppose because they became routine to me. I guess the reason I recall that first dinner so well is because it was important to me and I put so much effort into it. And I learned something from the short but pithy conversation that took place later.

"How was my dinner?" I asked William that evening, anxious for some small crumb of approval.

"How come you served plain, boiled potatoes?" he asked. "All the other women always serve mashed potatoes."

It was an answer that made me feel more like a rib than a woman and I fumed inwardly. Was a woman good for nothing except to wait on the men? Was it necessary to cook everything exactly as they wanted it?

The answer was yes, of course. Yes, if you wanted to be considered as good a cook as the other women in the neighborhood. Yes, if you wanted your husband to be proud of you. For want of a bowl of hot, mashed potatoes my culinary battle had been lost, apparently. It was a mistake that I never made again.

It required several sessions of cooking for hay men and threshers before I was fully competent to get a meal cooked and served on time with no embarrassing hitches. Cooking for threshers was more work than cooking for hay men because there were bigger crews, usually twelve or thirteen men, and a threshing crew might be at our place for two or three days. In our neighborhood, we were expected to take lunch to the field about four in the afternoon, so by the time the dinner dishes were done it was time to start preparing these lunches, plus gallons of iced tea, all of which had to be carried to the car, hauled to the field, and set out where the men could get to it.

However, taking lunch to the field was less work than having the men come to the house for a complete supper, which is what they did in some other neighborhoods. We women were thankful for even small favors in those days, so we were grateful for that.

When I got the mechanics well in hand I found that I actually enjoyed cooking for all those men and I strove, not merely to fill them up, but to cook the kinds of foods they liked. Devil, properly stoked with the right combination of green and dry wood, was equal to the task. I arose early and made a big batch of yeast rolls and brought them to the table piping hot. Using my mother's recipe for baked beans, I made a big panful, seasoned with brown sugar, onions, and tomato and layered on top with thick bacon. There was always a roast or fried chicken, lots of gravy, and two or three kinds of pie, so a man was sure to find one that suited his fancy.

While the men ate I hovered over them, waiting on their merest whim and blatantly hoping for a compliment. I remember with fondness one man, a bachelor, who ran the threshing machine and got to eat at everyone's table for miles around every summer. He used to tell me that he liked to eat at our house because my cooking was exactly like his mother's.

"Exactly," he would say, reaching for another hot roll.

It was enough to send me back to the kitchen wagging my tail.

Winter in the "Taj Mahal"

CORN HUSKING was, and still is, the biggest job on a farm — even with modern machinery it remains a big job. Looking back on it, one wonders how farmers ever managed to do it by hand. The task, in retrospect, seems almost insurmountable. Only two rows could be husked at a time and each ear had to be handled separately. The husker grabbed the ear with both hands, his left stripping off the husk, his right snapping the naked ear off the stalk and giving it a toss toward the wagon. A good husker worked with clock-like precision and his speed could be gauged by the staccato beat of the ears against the bangboard.

It was apparent from the very start that getting the corn in was going to be a hard job that first year. October was cold and wet. By early November the ground froze and we were getting a little snow. But the sun was still warm enough to melt the snow and this made the hills slick and hazardous for man and horse alike.

William got up earlier than usual so he could have the chores done and be on his way to the field by daylight. Still bleary eyed and sleepy, I would watch him pull out of the yard with Bud and Beauty hitched to the empty wagon. Fortified by pork sausage and a dozen pancakes, he would be whistling a tuneless but happy ditty. The horses, their breath making frosty clouds around their heads, would be trotting along because that light wagon was as nothing to their great strength. I knew that I could expect them back shortly before noon. But William would no longer be whistling and Bud and Beauty would be

Bud — too bad he couldn't recognize himself
for the hero he was

leaning into their collars with heads down and muscles straining to bring the results of their morning's labor to the crib.

One day when the wagon was heavily loaded, it became necessary to bring the load up over a short but steep hill. It was slow going and the horses had a hard time getting a foothold. Beauty's feet slipped out from under her and she fell to her knees. Bud, sensing a crisis, responded immediately. He stopped and strained forward, locking his legs in muscles of iron and immobilizing the load until Beauty could get to her feet again. Bud was quite a horse, William told me when he came in to dinner that day.

"How did Beauty react?" I asked.

"She got a little nervous. But she got up as soon as she could and moved right back in place to help Bud," he said.

"What would have happened if Bud hadn't been able to hold the load?" I inquired.

"Then I would have had to let him back down the hill until I could have turned the wagon at right angles so he could hold it. But that might not have worked, either. The load might have upset or Beauty might have gotten tangled up in the harness and been injured. It's hard to tell what would have happened if it hadn't been for Bud."

Good old Bud. A lot of horses in similar circumstances would have fought until they freed themselves from their harness. By keeping his cool Bud might have saved Beauty from a broken leg. At the very least he had saved William from having to scoop a load of corn off the ground. It was too bad he couldn't recognize himself for the hero he was.

It was almost Christmas before William got the corn out of the field that year and the landlord, upon being apprised of this fact, came out to see it. William was not home when he came and, after he'd walked around the cribs and admired the yellow ears that were almost as good as money in the bank, he came to the house to talk to me. He was obviously pleased over the size of the corn crop. It proved that the ground was rich, he said. (He pronounced the word as "reech.")

I assured him that we were just as happy as he was about the crop. I suggested it was probably because of the fertilizer left by the sheep the previous renter had.

"Yes, yes. Reech soil. Good farm. Reech soil," he answered.

Then he took a tour of the house, something he never failed to do when he came out. While he sauntered through the kitchen, the dining room, and the living room, his sharp eyes didn't miss a thing. I was never able to understand these inspection trips; they made me uncomfortable and I considered them an unnecessary intrusion. The only possible explanation for them was that he loved the farm and every stick and stone on it and loved the house the same way. It all belonged to him, didn't it? Therefore, he was privileged to examine it. He always made these tours with such utter innocence and such remarkable casualness that it was hard to ascribe any lesser motives to his actions.

Then, too, he always took time to admire our toddler. And it's pretty hard to complain about a man who pats your toddler on the head and tells you what a fine boy you have there.

"You having any trouble keeping warm these days?" he asked.

"Not yet," I answered.

"Yes, yes. Reech soil. Warm house," he purred.

At supper that evening I told William about the landlord's visit. "He was really happy about the corn crop," I said.

"I expect he was. I bet he never expected to see both cribs full," William replied. "Did he take his usual tour of the house?"

"Of course. You know he's as proud of this house as if it were the Taj Mahal," I remarked. "That's what he acts like—like it's a palace. He literally beams whenever he looks at it. He asked me today if we had been able to keep warm enough and I told him that we had been."

I quoted the landlord's comment on the rich soil and warm house.

"The soil might be rich but I doubt if the house is warm," William answered. "This house is old and the doors and windows don't fit well. We won't know how cold it will be until the weather gets down below zero. And we're sure to have some of that. After all, the worst of the winter is still ahead of us."

William was right. The worst of the winter was still ahead of us. And a Taj Mahal we had not.

Shortly after Christmas, winter descended with unbelievable ferocity. Scarcely had one blizzard blown itself out when another came along. Snow banks continued to grow until the cars on the road were no longer visible from the kitchen window. The cold winds lunged and tore at the house savagely. We discovered that the doors and windows were even looser than we thought they were. I tore up strips of cloth and paper and stuffed them into the cracks with a thin-bladed knife and this helped somewhat. But there was always a telltale movement of the curtains which belied my efforts.

We kept the heating stove and Devil going full blast all day and William banked both the fires before he went to bed. However, he refused to get up in the night and build them up again, which is what I had been telling him he ought to do. But he said he didn't want a fire getting out of control in the night and burning the house down around us while we slept, to which I invariably replied that I would just as soon burn to death as freeze to death.

In the mornings we would find that our breath had condensed into frost on the blankets under our noses. I woke up stiff and sore from having lain rigidly in the same place all night, afraid to move lest I have to warm up a different place in the bed. The water pail and teakettle always had ice frozen in them in the mornings.

I could not see how anyone could be so miserable and still survive. I was appalled at the thought of spending weeks and perhaps months of each year in such discomfort. But we were not alone. Almost all our neighbors were in the same boat. We were living in a central heatingless, electric blanketless world, and we survived only because we knew we had to. Anyway, it would have been a rotten time of year to die.

Our toddler began these winter nights in his crib, bundled in multiple diapers, multiple shirts, long stockings, and a nightgown with drawstrings at the bottom and over his hands. He had a knitted cap that came down over his ears and tied under his chin. Nothing showed but his face. I tucked his covers around him and secured them under the mattress of his crib.

Nevertheless, he always managed to fight his way out of this maternal strait jacket in a few hours and wake up crying, arms and legs flailing in the cold. Changing an icy diaper at two in the morning was an ordeal for both of us. When it was over and he was sufficiently waterproofed and wrapped in warm blankets again I took him to bed with us, cuddling him up in the fashion of mothers since time immemorial.

I was sure that he would get pneumonia long before spring but, strangely enough, he thrived in this Spartan environment.

Clad in a pair of minute coveralls and a warm sweater, he rode around in his kiddie car most of the day. He couldn't talk yet but his gestures were eloquent. When he pushed himself out to the kitchen and reached up to the table I knew what he wanted—a thick slice of homemade bread with plenty of butter and sugar on top, something I remembered eating as a child. This would please him mightily and he would take the bread, give me a sugary smile, and scoot away.

William agreed that the winter was pretty bad, but he was cheerful about it. It took him almost all day to fight his way through the snow and get the chores done. He had to build a fire in the tank to thaw the ice so the livestock could drink, and the short-legged hogs couldn't make it through the snow so he had to carry water to them. All the barn creatures had to have extra bedding at night. The strawpile was outdoors so he had to carry big forkfuls of straw into the barn. Not only this, but he tended the hens, whose egg production dropped sharply as a result of the weather. And he carried all the fuel and water for the house.

The horses didn't mind being out in the snow if they could find a place where they were out of the wind. But the poor cows were obviously miserable, and they went back to the barn the first chance they got. I worried about the barn creatures until William told me there was no need to. "It's very comfortable in the barn at night with all that animal heat," he said, which was a comforting thought in itself.

William went to town to take the cream and eggs in and buy the groceries, while I stayed behind to keep the home fires burning. As the winter wore on I became as fidgety as an Eskimo squaw at Point Barrow with no mukluks to chew on. I yearned desperately to go to town so William offered to stay home and tend the fires and Donny.

"But I think you're making a mistake," he said. "The road is icy and you haven't had any experience driving on ice."

"How am I going to get any experience unless I do it?" I asked.

"You might slide off into the canyon," he warned.

I retorted that none of the other women seemed to be afraid of the canyon and I wasn't, either. He said he could understand my desire to get away for awhile but he added that he thought I'd picked a helluva time to go, and he was right about that.

The canyon was a forty-foot-deep drainage ditch at the bottom of a long hill and the bridge over it was wide but it had no railings. Not only that, but you had to make a sharp turn just before you crossed the bridge. There was always the possibility that you would come down off that steep hill, slither at the turn, lose control of the car, and slide into the canyon. It had been done. The whole thing—the long hill, the sharp turn, the railless bridge—could only have been conceived by an engineer with strong homicidal tendencies. And it was this road that I was determined to drive on.

I drove carefully and everything was going all right until I started down that last treacherous hill with the canyon at the bottom. Suddenly, the car began to turn sideways and I did the worst thing I could have done. I put the brakes on. The car spun completely around in the road. I was now pointed toward home and that is where I went.

It did my ego no good when I met Bee Bagley on her way to town. She was wearing her red velvet hat with the pheasant wing in the front and she waved cheerily to me as we met. I realized that she had me bested. She not only had a red velvet hat with a pheasant wing in front, but she had driving experience and courage as well. The icy road and the canyon held no terrors for her. She took it all in stride.

"I thought you knew better than to set your brakes when you were driving on the ice," William told me later.

"I do know better—now," I answered.

So went our first winter in the Taj Mahal. We would have a lot more winters just like it and some of them were worse. The best I could do was put myself into a sort of grin-and-bear-it holding pattern until spring.

Our entertainment consisted of an occasional card party and the women's club tried to meet once a month. But both of these brief interludes of pleasure were contingent upon the weather. Certainly, nobody wanted to venture far from home when it was snowing or the roads were drifting. Television hadn't been invented yet. Radios ran on batteries and the inclination was to conserve those batteries as long as one could, so the radio didn't get used very often.

Poets speak glowingly of the old-fashioned winters, of the blazing log, the soft, romantic gleaming of lamplight, the contentment of a family gathered around the welcoming hearth. But I always figured those poets hadn't ever tried an old-fashioned winter, and if they had they might not have liked it.

We had no blazing log. What we had was an ugly heating stove. It made a lot of soot and ashes and seldom heated the corners of the room. To get any comfort at all you had to pull your chair up close to the stove, where your front half practically got scorched while the cold chills were still running up and down your spine. And anybody who has ever tried to read or knit by the dubious light from a kerosene lamp can tell you how exasperating it is.

However, there was one thing that certainly helped to keep us on an even keel during those long winters—our "party" line. There were fourteen families on this same telephone line, strung throughout the countryside like so many pumpkins on a vine. Our phones hung on the wall and had to be cranked. Each household had its own ring, a combination of long rings and short rings. Ours was one long and three shorts and when I heard it I raced to the telephone with all the alacrity of a well-trained fire horse.

If you wanted to hear somebody else's conversation, all you had to do was lift the receiver and listen. A few of the men listened in and practically all of the women did. Of course, the sound of the receiver being lifted caused a little click on the line, but that posed no problem because nobody knew where the click had come from, so our anonymity was preserved.

Often the conversation was mere woman talk, a pleasant and inconsequential chatter calculated to while away the time. But we also got a lot of important news that way, like when a baby had been born or someone was ill or there had been an accident. That's how we found out about Pearl Harbor.

If there was a real emergency you practically cranked the phone off the wall in one, long, continuous ring. That brought everybody to the phone, day or night. If we'd had a blizzard and the roads were drifted full when a doctor was needed, that call would bring men on the double. With five or six men it did not take long to shovel enough snow for the doctor to get through.

There were always certain stretches of road that drifted badly every winter. The men knew exactly where these were, of course, and the farmers who lived nearest these trouble spots knew what their responsibilities were. Sometimes the drifts were too much for a tractor and a homemade drag (two planks nailed together in a V-shape), but a good team of horses would usually bring the drag through. If not—the shovels!

The party line could be a nuisance, especially if you got a call that you wished other people couldn't hear. But it was a godsend in many ways. It kept us in touch with the rest of the world, no matter how many blizzards we had. And we knew that if we needed help it would not be long in coming.

During the spring that followed our first winter in the Taj Mahal we finally got electricity. We had been told to keep our light switches on so we would know when the power coursed through the lines for the first time. It was a great moment when all at once the lights came on and every room in the house lit up in a blaze of splendor. All we had were ceiling lights, but you cannot imagine what that simple drop cord and naked light bulb meant to us.

Now we could read in the evenings. I vacuumed up all the dust I could see and some I couldn't see. I carried the wretched sad irons to the attic and hoped I would never have to use them again. (I would.) I washed for three days straight, with no backaches and no complaining. William was just as happy as I was, for now he had lights in the barn and no longer had to carry a lantern to chore. We bought a new refrigerator and now the butter didn't melt and the milk didn't sour. I whipped up a lot of frozen desserts out of our own cream and eggs. The ice cubes tinkled invitingly in our glasses.

It was wonderful. Electricity made life much more pleasant and my work a great deal easier. Of course, as I pointed out to William, we hadn't caught up with the Cretans yet, who had had running water in their houses four thousand years ago. But the electricity was certainly a step in the right direction.

Beauty and Other Beasts

WE were all devoted to our horses in those days—had to
be, for they were the only source of power we had. A few
of the more well-to-do farmers had tractors. But we didn't, so
everything depended upon the two bays—Bud and Beauty—
and the two grays—Dick and Dan. William, as it turned out,
was uncommonly devoted to Beauty.

Bob Irving had a greater investment in horses than anyone
else, for he had several brood mares and a stallion named King
and he raised colts to sell. The first time I saw one of those
velvety-nosed colts I fell in love with it and wanted one for my
own. And that ambition could easily be realized. We had a
mare and there was King, readily available less than two miles
away. It seemed perfectly logical to me.

I knew that all that stood between me and one of those
colts was William. Casually, so as not to alarm him, I brought
up the subject. He didn't say yes but he didn't say no and I had
lived with him long enough to know that when he said no he
really meant yes but didn't want to give in just yet. So I kept up
the pressure for several days, but I could see that he wasn't
going to give in this time.

Beauty was an exceptionally fine looking mare, he said,
and he had no intentions of letting her have a colt and lose her
shape in the process. His reasoning was a little hard for me to
follow, especially since I was pregnant at the time. But there it
was, and nothing I said could make him change his mind. He
didn't even answer when I asked a perfectly innocent question
about whether or not mares got stretch marks.

It was apparent that nothing short of an act of God would give me that colt. Brick Nelson said he'd had an act-of-God colt once. "That mare of mine had never even been near a stallion," he declared vehemently. "I never even let her out of the pasture. Wasn't no stud for miles around anyway. But she showed up with a dandy colt one day. I never did get it figured out."

I was disappointed, not only for myself but for Beauty, who would never know the joys of having her own knobby-kneed colt frisking at her side. But after William explained the drawbacks in raising a colt I began to see why he was so adamantly opposed to the idea. We didn't need another horse and a colt could not be sold until it was broken to harness, he said, and this could be a dangerous process. Not only that, but while the colt was very young it would have to go to the field with Beauty so it could nurse.

"Can you imagine the trouble Dan might cause if there was a colt running around him in the field while I was trying to plow?" William asked.

It was a good point. Dan was skittish enough as it was and the presence of a colt would only make him worse.

All four horses were needed to do the plowing in the spring or fall. William put Bud and Beauty in the middle on the theory that they were older and better trained and that the relatively young grays would be less likely to cause trouble if they were split up. Dick always took his place beside Bud and stood quietly while he was being hitched. But Dan was something else again. You could get him hitched at his head all right, but then he would move his rear around so that he stood at right angles to the other horses and he would stay there, snorting ominously and pawing the ground like a bull. No amount of yelling would make him take his proper position. William always had to shove his backside into line. This would get Dan all excited and he would roll his eyes and snort and prance up and down like a three-quarter ton rocking horse.

The trouble with Dan was that he didn't seem to know he was a work horse. He was a full grown three year old and he should have been putting his coltishness behind him, but he never did take life seriously. With his long neck it was easy for him to reach over a fence for a tempting bit of grass on the other side. Sometimes he just straddled a fence, oblivious to the sharp barbs on the wire that were no more than the prick of a pin to his thick hide. He had a mean streak in him, too, and wasn't above delivering a swift kick to a fellow horse or to one of the defenseless milk cows.

In the barn he was a veritable Houdini, who used his lips and tongue to untie his halter rope. Sometimes we would be roused out of our sleep by loud whacks coming from the barn and then we would know that he was on the loose again. Either he was kicking the barn in the sheer joy of freedom, or his prowlings had disturbed one of the other horses, who had kicked at him, missed, and landed a blow on the stall instead. Dan was a maverick and he knew it. What's more—he didn't give a damn. Being hitched to machinery was an ignominy. Working was something for the less-spirited horses, like the docile Dick, the phlegmatic Bud, or the nervous but tractable Beauty.

Nevertheless the plowing that spring had gone off quite well and William thought all that hard work might have settled Dan down a bit. However, William wanted to use two cultivators to plow the corn and to do this the teams would have to be split up. Our young nephew Rolly offered to run one cultivator, and he also wanted to drive Dick and Dan.

All went well during the first morning. The grays plodded faithfully along, crossing the field on two rows and coming back on two more. Dan seemed to be on his best behavior, walked calmly at a steady pace, and planted his dinner-plate sized feet pretty much where they were supposed to go.

But coming home at noon all hell broke loose. William had taken the lead while Rolly followed a short distance behind. Suddenly Dan spooked. He reared high on his hind legs and came down running. There wasn't anything Dick could do but run along with him. The reins were torn out of Rolly's hands and the cultivator was jerked out from under him. He shouted a warning to William, who saw the grays bearing down on him and jumped to safety.

Within seconds, the grays were upon Bud and Beauty, leaping in between them and pulling one cultivator over the top of the other. Bud and Beauty broke loose and ran for home. Dick and Dan—forced to run up a fairly steep hill and burdened with the weight of two cultivators—eventually slowed down, and the men caught up with them. William unhitched them and drove them home, talking soothingly to calm them down. Dick did manage finally to collect his equine wits, but Dan was still plunging wildly when he got to the yard.

Except for broken harnesses, there was no real harm done, although William would almost certainly have been seriously injured or possibly killed if he hadn't jumped off the cultivator in time. William had never really trusted Dan and he trusted him a lot less now. He was very watchful of the grays after that, drove them himself, and kept them under tight rein.

Brick Nelson, who fancied himself quite a horseman (although not so great that his horses didn't have cockleburrs in their tails the year around) thought William had made a great mistake by not beating the horses that day. "You should have hitched them to a wagon and run them as fast as they could go, whipping them every foot of the way," he said. "That would have taught them a lesson." But William did not believe in this sort of thing and I was glad he didn't. It was Dan who caused the trouble, he said, and the other horses could scarcely be blamed for doing what they had done.

William was always eager to get along with our neighbors, which helped to explain why he was so patient with Brick Nelson's bull, who spent practically all of one summer at our place. Farmers are supposed to keep their livestock behind fences or in barn lots. They are not supposed to run willy-nilly around the countryside. This is especially true of a bull, who may be dangerous to strangers.

As it is with everything else on the farm, there is a standard approach to the problem of a stray animal. If the creature is familiar, you call your neighbor on the phone and tell him that his cow, or his bull, or whatever it is, is at your place and you think he would like to know. He will thank you for the information and will come and get the animal and the incident will end there. However, if the same animal is back the next day, you will begin to think that your neighbor is a bit careless. And if the same thing happens every day for a week you will realize that you have a real problem on your hands.

How are you going to convince that valued neighbor to keep his livestock at home without being offensive about it? One way you can do this is simply ignore the whole thing, allow the wayward animal to visit you whenever he feels like it, and hope that your neighbor will mend his ways — and his fences — in time. William thought this was the best solution to the problem of Brick's bull.

One morning I was standing over Devil washing dishes when I heard a snuffing sound at the screen door. There, his fearsome head framed by the flimsy wood around the screen, stood the biggest, blackest, most sinister looking bull I had ever seen in my life. He had huge horns that must have spanned five feet from tip to tip. But he didn't seem to be angry, merely curious. He kept smelling the screen door, making gentle whoofing sounds as he ran his nose up and down on it. I recognized him at once, for I had seen him in the pasture with Brick's cows.

Even though he appeared friendly, I decided he would have to go. I clattered the screen door in his face several times and yelled, "Get out of here!" But he didn't understand English and was not about to let a mere woman chase him away. He continued to stand there, whoofing affably, running his nose up and down the door and switching his tail in a vain effort to chase the flies away. With this he wasn't having much luck. He had a whole colony of flies across his shoulders where his tail wouldn't reach and they were scampering all over this safe conduct zone looking for some pierceable hide. Some of them had found their places and were firmly anchored, drunk and groggy with rich bull blood. For this, I pitied him.

I yelled at the bull again but he continued to stand at my door, gazing at me with limpid, purplish eyes. I went back to the kitchen and watched him through the window. He finally left the door and ambled about the house yard for awhile. Then he ran through the willow trees east of the house, trying to rid himself of the torturing flies. I knew when I heard the fence creak that he had jumped over into the alfalfa field.

After that the bull paid us frequent visits. It was a rare week when he appeared less than twice. And he was sneaky. I couldn't see how an animal of that size could move so quietly. He was like a cat. No hoofbeat could be heard. No twig snapped. Unless there were other cattle around he seldom bellowed. He seemed to materialize out of nowhere and often the first warning of his presence was his arrival at my screen door.

Blissfully unaware that alfalfa could make him bloat up and die, he continued to eat the stuff anyway. (There is only one way to save a bloated animal and that is to plunge a knife down between his ribs so the gas can escape.) I used to envision the bull lying on his back in the alfalfa field with his legs stiff in the rigors of death. It was a happy thought but it never came to pass. He just wasn't the bloaty type.

Brick always came promptly when he was called. He didn't seem one bit embarrassed about having to be called so many times. But I was angry about the whole thing. I complained to William that Donny and I were virtual house prisoners. I threatened to call Brick and tell him off. This alarmed William, who warned me not to do it.

"Brick is hotheaded," he said. "If you start complaining he probably won't help me put up my hay. Anyway, men don't like to have neighbor women tell them what to do."

"Or maybe where to go," I said acidly.

One day William gave me a short but pithy lecture on bull psychology. "If you are outdoors when he comes, don't panic. Under no circumstances should you run. Any sudden movement might alarm him and make him chase you," he said.

"What'll I do if he chases me anyway?" I whined.

"If he knocks you down lie perfectly still. Don't move a muscle. Don't even blink your eyes. Then he will think you are dead and he won't trample you or gore you."

"If that bull knocks me down I won't have to play dead. I'll be dead," I said.

"Well, as usual, you are making a mountain out of a molehill," William replied. "Brick says that bull isn't dangerous and he ought to know. Lolly and the kids are around him all the time and they aren't afraid of him."

I made some smart remark about taking up bull leaping for a sport, like the Cretans had done four thousand years ago. But the humor was lost on William, who thought I was being foolish to get so nerved up over such an inoffensive animal.

However, his nonchalance suddenly disappeared one evening when he tried to come out of the barn after doing the milking. The bull had been in the barn lot when William went to do the chores. He had seemed docile enough then and had made no objections when the cows were taken into the barn to be milked. But it required an hour to do the milking and during that time the bull's mood changed. When William opened the door he was met by a furious bull, who was pawing the ground and had his head down ready to charge. Sensing that the bull was angry because he had been separated from the cows so long, William turned them back into the barn lot, whereupon the bull quieted down.

William didn't want to take any unnecessary chances, however, so he left the barn through a rear door, lifted the milk pails over the fences, and came to the house by a circuitous route. For him, this was the moment of truth. He wasn't going to put up with it any longer, he grouched when he got to the house. He was going to tell Brick in no uncertain terms that he was going to have to keep that so-and-so of a bull home where he belonged.

Brick came immediately, clattering into the yard in his rusty old pickup, his ten-year-old daughter beside him. By this time, of course, the bull appeared to be as harmless as a kitten. William went down to have a talk with Brick, who started right off saying that he didn't know what he was going to do with that devil, that no matter how many times he fixed the fences the bull went through them.

"Some animals are like that," William conceded, still unwilling to offend Brick.

"Eunice," Brick commanded, "you go down there and bring that bull out in the yard."

"I'll open the gate for her," William offered.

"Hell, no! Let her do it herself. She's done it before," Brick answered.

So that prepubescent snippet of a girl obediently jumped out of the pickup, opened the heavy gate, circled around the bull and brought him to where her father wanted him, having also shut the gate, of course. William couldn't understand it.

"How come a girl can make him mind when he was ready to attack me only a few minutes ago?" he asked.

"That's because you was scared of him," Brick said. "Bulls can smell fear. But there ain't nothin' to be afraid about. I raised that bull from a calf and he wouldn't hurt a flea."

"I'd appreciate it if you'd keep him home. My wife is afraid of him," William said.

79

"Well, she's a town woman," Brick remarked, as if that explained everything.

It was quite awhile before the bull came back again and I had begun to think that Brick finally had him corralled. I was no longer afraid to go to the Necessary lest I be besieged therein. Carrying water was almost pleasurable and I whipped out to the woodpile with a happy heart. Donny was freed from his maternal yo-yo. He was now allowed to take his wagon to the sandbox and he spent many happy hours hauling sand from the box, where it should have been, to the sidewalk, where it shouldn't have been.

Later that summer, William bought some heifers to feed out. These were young cattle weighing five hundred pounds, to which we would add another four or five hundred by feeding them corn, hay, and protein supplement. They ate and they drank and they grew and became beautiful to behold. They looked at us with gentle, unknowing eyes, unaware of the fate that awaited them. They were "open" heifers. That is, they weren't pregnant. And it was our job to keep them that way until they went to market.

The cattle did a great deal of bellowing just before feeding time, and Brick's bull, far away in his pasture, heard them and came to see what all the fuss was about. And he liked what he saw. Here was a whole yard full of youthful females awaiting his attention. It was against his principles to have an unbred cow or heifer around and he patrolled every foot of the fence looking for a way to get to them. The giddy heifers were entranced by his attention and they patrolled the inside of the fence right along with him. Angry and frustrated, he pawed the ground, sending up little puffs of dust around his peppering hooves.

And he bellowed! Surely, there is no more menacing sound on earth than that of a bellowing bull. It is defiant, sonorous; it resonates from his cavernous chest. It is a fearsome yet fascinating sound and, listening to it, one feels an awe like that primitive man must have known as he crouched in his cave listening to the roaring of wild beasts without.

The bull put on quite a show on several occasions, but finally the heifers got used to him and they no longer ran to the fence to greet him. If none of them was in an amorous mood he ignored them, too, and simply wandered around the house yard to amuse himself. Brick would come after him if we called or if he discovered he was missing—whichever came first. As for the bull, he must have been thoroughly confused by this time. Where did he belong anyway?

William discussed the situation with Bob Irving and they agreed something would have to be done. Bob said he knew of a way to get rid of the bull once and for all. When the bull appeared next time, I was to call Bob and tell him that we had a "visitor." Bob would come at once, he said, although he didn't explain what he would do when he got there.

We should have known that the fence would not hold against the bull forever, and it didn't. William was in the barn when he heard the snapping of posts and the wrenching of barbed wire. He knew then that what he feared most had happened. The bull was in the barn lot with the heifers.

And there was one heifer that was susceptible to his charms. He pursued her relentlessly but the moment when she would stand still for him had not yet come upon her. The pair of them went around and around the barn lot, she demurring in maidenly modesty, he determined to put an end to her virginity once and for all. The other heifers were running along with them, pushing and shoving each other and bellowing in excitement. At the house, I was alerted by the noise. I took one look and decided that if there was ever a time Bob was needed, it was now. When he came, he was armed with a shotgun.

"You're not going to kill the bull, are you?" I asked in alarm.

"No. But I'm going to fill him so full of buckshot that he'll never come back again," Bob replied.

The first thing the men had to do was separate the bull from the heifers, so they drove them to one corner of the feedlot. Next, they had to turn the bull away from his enamorata, whom he was following with stubborn singularity of purpose. The men went between the bull and the heifer and he backed off. Then the reason for all of this dawned on him and he lowered his head, pawed the ground, and roared with rage. The men kept forcing him back and suddenly he ran for the alfalfa field, going through the fence like it was made of paper.

This was the opportunity Bob had been waiting for, and he shot the bull in his retreating backside. Angrier than ever, the bull turned and charged Bob, who climbed up on the straw-stack and yelled at William to take refuge in the barn. It was one man against the bull now and I marveled at Bob's courage, for it looked like the bull was going to climb the strawstack to get to him. Bob waited until he was quite close, then shot him in the shoulders. The bull roared in pain and conceded defeat. He turned and ran for home.

The next day the bull attacked Brick, who saw him coming, fortunately, and managed to escape. Brick knew any bull that attacks once is quite likely to do it again, so he had the animal sent to slaughter.

This development caused a crisis of conscience in me, a lesser crisis for William, and no crisis at all for Bob, who insisted that both Brick and the bull had gotten exactly what they deserved. Nobody ought to let a bull go wherever he chose, Bob said. Therefore we were justified in taking any measures to protect ourselves. All of this was true, of course. But it had been only by the grace of God that the bull went after Brick instead of Lolly or one of the children, and for that we were grateful.

However, I was somewhat saddened over the demise of the big black bull, with his ivory horns and purplish eyes, and his strange propensity for whoofing at my screen door. I consoled myself with the thought that he was already old, and the slaughter house would have been his eventual fate in any case. We probably hadn't shortened his life more than a year or two.

One thing is certain: there is a need for constant vigilance when working among farm animals. Many a man has been injured or killed by a supposedly gentle bull. Cows do not get angry very often, usually only when someone comes between them and their calves. Here again, the female is conceded to be the deadlier of the species. A bull will keep his head down and go in a straight line when he charges, so it is possible to allow him to get fairly close and then jump out of his way. But a cow is more crafty. She keeps her head up and her eyes upon her victim when she charges, so it is much more difficult to escape from her.

So it can be said that cows are more reasonable. When a cow is angry it is because someone has posed a threat to her offspring, to which she is intensely devoted and which she will fight to protect. But bulls need no such lofty excuses. They can work themselves into a blind, earth-pawing, roaring rage within minutes and nobody is ever sure just why.

And bulls develop this tendency at an early age. One time when William was working in the barn, I carried Jimmy, who was a baby then, and went to see what he was doing. A one-year-old bull calf saw us coming, pawed the ground, lowered his head and charged toward us. I screamed for William, who came to the rescue. But I was much more careful thereafter to avoid this ill-tempered juvenile, who was obviously determined to assert male domination over the barnyard long before he reached adulthood.

Of Many Things

THERE were many changes in our lives during those first three years on the farm. The most significant one for us was the birth of our second son, Billy. Donny, meanwhile, had grown into a precocious two year old who could disappear in minutes. Once I found him sitting up on top of the corn crib. So my days were spent running in and out of the house, trying to keep an eye on him and take care of an infant at the same time.

We had become close friends with Bob and Alice Irving. She and I were very compatible and her friendship added a new dimension to my life. It was a great disappointment when they moved away. After having farmed the hills so many years, Bob was anxious to have some level land, and we could understand that. But I felt like I was back to square one as far as a woman-to-woman relationship was concerned.

These were the war years and, as it happens during every war, farm prices shot up and we were grateful for that. But as we read of the terrible battles and of the sufferings of innocent people everywhere, and as the young men we knew went off to war — perhaps never to return — we took small pleasure in our extra dollars. The first young man from our town to die in the war was his parents' only child, and their pain became our pain.

Our nephew Rolly joined the Navy with a personal score to settle, because his brother John had been taken prisoner at Corregidor. It was almost three months before his distraught mother received a postal card from him, saying that he was at Camp Cabanatuan, in the Philippines. Each day I thought about him and worried about him. It was to be three long years before he came home.

We knew that we were very fortunate to be living on the farm during these troubled times. We took satisfaction in knowing that we were helping to feed the world's hungry and that without the American farmer, there would be much more suffering.

One of the changes in our lives was subtle but nonetheless meaningful: we were no longer considered a curiosity in the neighborhood. During our first year we had been met by a barrage of questions concerning our motives in coming to the farm. What fool notion, the neighbors would ask, had made us give up the certainty of a weekly paycheck for the dubious security of a farm where there was absolutely no way of knowing how much money you were going to have at the end of the year? They couldn't understand this, and they inferred that only an idiot would be foolish enough to forsake the town for the country. But they knew now that we were here to stay and they no longer questioned our wisdom in coming. It was a great feeling to know that they had accepted us. At long last, we were considered genuine farmers.

Some of those extra dollars went to good use. We replaced the old range with a new cooking stove. It had a commodious oven, a copper-lined reservoir, and the usual warming closet. I was delighted with it but I did not have it very long until I saw that I had simply swapped the old black Devil for a new white devil. I therefore dubbed him Satan. He required just as much fuel as the other one and made just as many ashes. I could still give Satan a talking to when he didn't heat up fast enough, but I didn't dare kick him because I didn't want to break his enamel. Besides, he didn't even have a belly button. Even so, it was fortunate that we bought a new stove. When we took old Devil out we discovered that he was badly rusted on the bottom, and it would have been only a matter of time before he set the kitchen floor afire.

Meanwhile, the hills weren't getting any flatter nor the horses any faster, and William yearned for a tractor. He guessed he'd go in and see Josh about it, he told me one morning.

Josh was our banker. His austere office, no bigger than a prison cell, was furnished only with a wide desk and big chair for himself, and a less comfortable chair for the squirming borrower. Here he kept a cautious finger on the economic pulse of the community. Going into that office was like going into a confessional. Here the chips were down. Here the truth was out.

Josh was a tall, gaunt man who must have been in his seventies. His nose was long and sharp and his cheeks sank in under prominent bones. He had a penetrating gaze calculated to strip bare the soul of any borrower. He seldom smiled. He bore an amazing resemblance to Abraham Lincoln and I never could quite shake the feeling that here, behind that desk, sat the Great Emancipator. And he didn't have the slightest desire to emancipate anybody.

I guess we were all in awe of Josh. He wielded so much power in our lives. We dreaded the displeasure in his sharp old eyes and we fretted when it came time to go over our notes and see where we stood — or more importantly, to find out where Josh thought we stood.

I knew the minute William came home that day that Josh had given him the nod. He was beaming when he came to the house. He'd bought a tractor, he told me.

"I think I got a bargain. It's been used three years but it's had good care. It ought to run at least a couple of years before it will need any repairs. It'll be brought out in a truck in the morning," he said.

And so it was that Gertrude came into our lives.

Her engine power was second to none, William assured me, and she was supposed to take snow and mud in stride. Her wheel rims were made of solid steel and they had wide cleats on them for better traction. A lot of her important parts were out in plain sight — things like gear shifts, and pistons, and various other things that I could not identify five minutes after William told me what they were. But they all looked very complex and imposing and seemed to fit in admirably with her radiator in front and her hood on top, and of course they were all connected in some mysterious way to her rear end where, if she developed trouble, it would be very expensive, William said.

Gertrude couldn't do the farming all by herself, of course. With her came a plow and a cultivator, which had to be attached to her front end. The cultivator weighed several hundred pounds and it was a hard job getting it attached to her chest. The levers that operated the cultivator were operated manually, a job that had to be done every time William turned around at the end of a row of corn.

You couldn't overwork horses. They had to have some rest at noon and they had to have one full day a week off. But Gertrude needed no rest. All you had to do was fill her up with gas and she was ready to go again.

Horses had intelligence and they knew when they were in disfavor. If you yelled at a horse or tugged at the reins, he reacted. There was, therefore, a sense of communication between William and the horses, no matter how exasperating that communication might be at times.

But Gertrude was a ton or two of cold steel. She knew nothing, felt nothing, and didn't give a damn about anything. No blow disturbed her. No curse moved her. If one small part of her innards was ailing — she was through. She sat there as unmoving as stone until you discovered what her trouble was. And Gertrude was sometimes recalcitrant about starting. Also, she had to be cranked.

One morning I heard William cranking and cranking. Between crankings he fiddled with various things, peeked at her carburetor, gave her more gas, and took some of her gas away. Nothing seemed to help. But William wasn't angry, merely puzzled. After a couple of hours, however, he had lost his patience and was giving Gertrude a verbal trouncing. I decided the least I could do was offer to help or give him some sympathy.

"What do you think is wrong?" I asked.

"If I knew what was wrong, I'd be fixing it," William countered sourly.

"Is there anything I could do to help?" I inquired.

"Nothin' you can do."

"I could crank once."

"No woman could crank this tractor. Besides, I've been cranking for two hours now and she still won't start."

"Just let me try," I persisted.

William bit off a little piece of his cigar and spat it out angrily. "I don't know what a woman could do. You don't even know how to crank a tractor. Remember, that was how Bob got his arm broken. He wasn't holding the crank right. You have to have your thumb and fingers on the same side of the handle so if Gertrude kicks she won't reverse her crank and hurt you."

"That's very interesting," I said. "This is once when the opposable thumb doesn't do any good."

"The what?"

"The opposable thumb. That's one reason why the human race has evolved so successfully — because we have an opposable thumb. It enables us to. . ."

William cut me short. "I didn't ask for a lecture. I'm just telling you how to crank this tractor."

He handed me the crank. Warily, I placed it in the shaft. I bent over, put my opposable thumb alongside my fingers like it was supposed to be, and gave the crank a turn. Miraculously, Gertrude sprang to life. Her pistons pumped up and down in perfect harmony. The little gizmo on top of her exhaust pipe chortled happily. She didn't cough, choke, or sputter. She just sat there, purring as smoothly as a kitten.

"Well, I'll be damned," William said. "I wonder what made her do that?"

"I guess she just needed a woman's touch," I said.

After we had used Gertrude for a few months, we found out things about her that we hadn't known before. For one thing, her wide steel wheels packed the ground too hard and made deeper ruts than the horses' hooves had. These ruts collected rain water that formed into small rivulets, gaining speed as they ran down the hills and causing erosion problems. Also, we found that it took more gas to energize a steel-wheeled tractor than one that ran on rubber.

Gertrude was touchy about getting water in the wrong places, too, and we found that the metal cap on her exhaust pipe did not keep rain out very well. This resulted in some unnecessary delays while William struggled to get the moisture out of her system. He solved this problem by putting a tin can over her exhaust. But if he forgot to take it off the next time he started her, she would blow that can ten feet into the air.

Gertrude wasn't fast and certainly could not compare with modern tractors in speed or efficiency. But she was dependable. Her strength was prodigious, her energy unflagging. She accepted each task with equanimity. There seemed to be no end to her stoical indifference to work. If Bud and Beauty got stuck with a big load of corn—never fear, Gertrude would come to the rescue. If the road was drifted full of snow—take heart, Gertrude would chew through it with her scoop. And if it rained day after day until the planting season was dangerously shortened—do not fret. Gertrude would roar into action, trundling up and down the hills with dogged persistence until the crops were in.

Later on, we bought rubber tires for Gertrude and a buzz saw that fitted across her chest and enabled us to saw a wagon load of wood in an hour or two. She had little ills from time to time, of course, and once she did have a severe problem with her rear end, which did cost a great deal to repair. But she was an admirable substitute for the work horses who were now used only to pick corn or put up hay. We would have a much handsomer and much more efficient tractor later on. But I don't think anything ever brought as much satisfaction to William as Gertrude did.

Our relationship with our landlord was amicable during the six years we lived on his place. He came out once each week, looked the crops and buildings over, and sometimes offered suggestions. But basically, he left us alone, which is what we wanted. However, tenants are prone to think that landlords expect them to put up with too much and I was no exception. He could very easily have piped water into the house, but he didn't. The henhouse was in bad shape, but he refused to fix it. The roof leaked and in the winter my hens often had snow drifting down on their backs while they sat on the nests laying their eggs. The house had been newly papered when we moved in but he balked at buying any more wallpaper, so we had to buy it ourselves.

I put up with these things with what was a fair degree of patience most of the time. I really liked the landlord. But a perfectly innocent skunk almost brought about a fatal rupture in our relationship.

There were two wells on the farm, both powered by windmills and both pumping water into a cistern near the house, from which the water ran down to a hydrant at the bottom of the hill and then had to be carried back to the house. This was ignominy enough, but the wells were worse. Both were "dug" wells, about fifty feet deep and lined with bricks. I became suspicious of the wells as soon as I found out how the water would rise in them and would surely stagnate in their dank depths. So I was already uptight about the wells long before the advent of the skunk, whose crime lay not in being thirsty, but where he chose to get a drink. He fell into one of our wells. This happened because the bricks had begun to cave in.

The workmen came, pumped the well dry, removed the skunk and rebricked the well. They used new bricks for the lower two-thirds of the well where the water would be. But for the upper one-third they used the same bricks that had previously been used above the water line, because they could detect no odor on them.

But I could. When the water from that well came into the pipeline the odor was there, and when the teakettle boiled the aroma of skunk permeated the kitchen. I was as mad as the proverbial hornet. I swore that I would never use a drop of that water for dishwashing or cooking and certainly not for drinking. I insisted that we haul clean water in from the neighbors, which we did. I was in no mood to welcome the landlord next time he came out. I brought the subject of the water up immediately.

"I don't know what you are getting so all-fired fussed up about," he said. "That water is clean. It never touches any of the old bricks. You're too particular. There's no reason why you can't use it. There isn't anything wrong with it at all."

I said there was.

He said there wasn't.

He was mad.

I was madder.

I offered him a drink.

He wasn't thirsty.

Finally, the landlord left, after muttering darkly about not being able to tell a woman anything. William was shocked when he found out about our argument.

"Now you've done it," he said accusingly. "He'll probably make us move now."

Although it took several weeks, the odor did finally disappear from the water. I realized then that I could have been a little more tactful with the landlord. But he didn't make us move—probably because he hadn't taken that drink of water when I offered it to him.

Of Many Things

I suppose my outburst and the landlord's huffish response is a good example of the natural disaffinity that exists between landlords and tenants. They are seldom on the same wave length. If you talk to any tenant farmer he will tell you that he is bearing a heavy load of expenses, has a lot of money wrapped up in machinery, and has to do all the dirty work. A landlord will tell you that he has the cost of upkeep on the farm, has high land taxes to pay, and his investment is not paying much return.

Both landlord and tenant are telling the truth, but it is always difficult for them to see the other's viewpoint. After a period of years, resentment will build up to the point where the landlord is looking for another tenant, and the tenant is looking for a different landlord. A change will be made and, for a time, peace will reign. But it won't last forever and the process will have to be repeated, perhaps many times.

The ideal situation is for a farmer to own the land he farms, preferably having inherited it so he won't have to make payments on it. Barring this, the next best thing is an absentee landlord—one who lives so far away that he can't get back more than once or twice a year. Or else the tenant can be thankful he has a place to live and he can treat the farm like his own, in which case the two of them may develop a satisfying relationship that will endure for many years.

I fear we never did appreciate that first landlord like we should have, and what he did the last year we lived on his place proved to us that he was far more deserving and much more generous than we had given him credit for. He came to the house and talked seriously to us one day. He intended to sell the farm, he said, and because we had lived there six years, he thought we ought to have the first chance to buy it. He would make it easy for us, he went on . All he wanted was the interest and something on the principal each year. We would not need to make a down payment.

It was an offer we were not likely to have again—and we turned it down. It was one of the greatest mistakes we ever made in our lives, but we did not realize that then and would not realize it for many years.

However, we had what we thought were perfectly logical reasons for doing this. Because of the war, prices had been good. But it would be foolish to buy land on the basis of a false prosperity. I remembered how my father had done this and the anguish it had caused him when he lost his farm. The war was over now and we knew it would be only a matter of time until prices came down again. Both of us could clearly recall the depression years when farmers had their mortgages foreclosed or lost their farms because of unpaid taxes. If these painful days returned we did not want to be one of the unfortunate families to lose everything.

We knew that the farm would be sold to someone very soon, and it was. Fortunately, we found a place to go in the same neighborhood. William was pleased because he would have twice as much land and more pasture for the cattle. I was happy to be leaving the Taj Mahal behind. It would be good to have a change of houses, I thought.

We looked forward to our new home with renewed faith and confidence. William and I were only in our early thirties and we could anticipate many more years of farming. Our family was growing. Donny was six, Billy four. Both were healthy boys and we hoped they were having a happy childhood. Soon there would be another child, for I was expecting a baby in April.

March first — traditional moving day for farmers — was cold but sunny and almost all of the snow was gone. Several of our neighbor men came to help us move, bringing their wagons and hayracks. I had cooked breakfast on Satan and he was too hot to be handled. But the heating stove was taken over to the other house and when I got there Chris Bagley had a hot fire going in it. He inadvertently supplied the only humor in what was an otherwise long and difficult day. He had set my rolled-up kitchen rug near the stove and he was turning it around and around so the heat would get to it.

"I'm trying to get your linoleum warmed up so it won't crack when we lay it down," he explained.

"That's very kind and thoughtful of you," I said.

"Think nothin' of it," he answered. "I know how it is when a woman has to move. She's apt to get upset over the least little thing and then she takes it out on her husband. I know how mad my missus gets when her linoleum gets cracked. I was only trying to save William a little trouble...haw haw."

At the End of the Lane

So now we were living in the big, old house at the end of the lane, off the main road and away from everybody. Here we were to spend the next twelve years. Here I would learn to like solitude, and that was fortunate, because I had plenty of it.

The house was a jerry-built thing. It had begun as two large rooms built more than a hundred years ago, the new landlord told us. Indians had crept up to peek through its windows many times. This ancient nucleus had been added to over the years to accommodate the three generations of the same family that had lived there, often two generations at the same time. Five more rooms had been built on as the numerous children arrived. The rough old floors had known the tramp of many feet and the woodwork was scratched and dented. One wall in the dining room had a weak spot where the plaster was coming through the wallpaper. I repaired this by putting a large piece of tin over the hole, covering the tin with a strip of window shade, and papering over everything.

I should not have liked the house, but I did. Its large rooms and sprawling spaciousness appealed to me. No two rooms were the same size or the same shape. I felt that the house had character.

Once again, we were without electricity. There was some argument between the landlord and the previous renters as to how this situation came about. When the rural electric lines were first strung, the government had decreed that a farmer have a certain number of cattle or hogs or chickens to qualify for electricity. The previous renters declared that they had had enough livestock to meet the requirements. The landlord insisted they didn't, however, so he did not have the wiring done. Whether the tenants or the landlord had been right made little difference now. We were the ones to suffer over their foolish squabbling.

Water was more handy for me now, because the pump was only twenty feet from the kitchen door. The well was a hundred feet deep and it took a large pump with a long handle to bring water from a well that deep. When I counted the number of strokes of the pump handle I discovered that they had to be increased day after day. Today—it might be thirty-five strokes. Next week—fifty strokes. After that—who could tell?

I asked William about this one day. "The well is getting harder and harder to pump," I said. "I wonder what's wrong with it?"

"It's not the well, it's the leathers in the pump," William explained. "When the leathers get worn they let some of the water slip back into the well, so you have to pump more strokes to fill your pail."

I pointed out to William that the pump was not the only thing that would need new leathers if the situation was allowed to continue. He spoke to the landlord about it and the landlord dutifully called a repairman. By the time the repairman got there the pump was up to ninety-five strokes.

After the new leathers were put in, the pump literally gushed water and we could get a pailful with five or six strokes. But ever so slowly the leathers would deteriorate and the number of strokes required would grow daily. Sometimes I got uptight over the pump and swore that I would never carry another pail of water until new leathers were put in. But that was easier said than done. If I needed water when the pump was up to eighty or ninety strokes, there was nothing to do but hie myself out and get it.

I never mentioned the pump to the landlord, who had been a widower for thirty years and was therefore not accustomed to hearing a woman complain. I felt instinctively that he would resent complaining and probably wouldn't welcome my suggestions, either.

Anyway, our new landlord was not a man one talked to. He was a man one listened to.

His father and mother had owned the farm before him and he and all of his brothers and sisters had been born and brought up there. He was fanatically devoted to the old place. Although he confessed to never having liked farming—he had left home and gotten a job in the city as soon as possible—he was proud because he had been the only one in the family with the foresight and the money to buy out the other heirs.

Now he was retired and had time to work on the farm. And he had plans—lots of plans. A list of the fences he wanted to set, the buildings he wanted to repair, and the changes he wanted to make would have reached from here to El Paso. His determination was so evident, his enthusiasm so contagious, that we found ourselves caught up in his plans. His dream became our dream. He would gesture grandly toward some trees and explain how he meant to get them out of there, how he would dam up the creek so the cattle would have a better place to drink, how he would build up the road so it didn't drift full of snow in the winter. We listened attentively, and we could see it all just the way he had it planned out.

Young people are usually considered to be the dreamers. They are the ones who are often accused of being impractical and of having their heads in the clouds. But I have always thought the opposite is true. It is the old people who dream, for they see the years piling up and their lives slipping away. One short year doesn't mean much at the age of twenty and it isn't so important whether you accomplish a great deal with it or not. But one year becomes terribly important at the age of sixty. Suddenly, you begin to realize that there isn't much more time left, and that if you expect to do anything with your life it will have to be done soon.

That was the way it was with our landlord. In his youth he had hated the farm; in his maturity he had worked hard to pay for it; now he was sixty and full of dreams for the old place. We knew that when he sat down with his back against the barn and lit up his pipe, he was living out his dream. In his mind's eye it was all done: the fences were built; the horses were in their new stalls; the barn had a new roof; the cattle shed was braced up; and the new henhouse was already built near the lane that led to the pasture.

Almost always the house—if it got mentioned at all—was

mentioned last, as sort of an afterthought. And why not? A nice house was desirable but it was the barn, the hoghouse, and the fences that always took priority. But occasionally the landlord would look toward the house and say, "By gracious, I'll have to give that house a coat of paint one of these days!"

The house probably hadn't been painted for twenty years, maybe more. It was gray and weather beaten. The nails in the siding had rusted and worked loose and some of the boards were beginning to curl. It fairly shouted "look-at-us-we're-poor" to anybody who drove into the yard. But I tried not to think too much about that.

In spite of all its defects, I loved the old house. I seldom thought about its old gray siding or the patch on the dining room wall or the ugly cupboard in the kitchen. The house had a history of its own. So many people had belonged to it at one time or another. In its youth it had lured Indians to its lamp-lit windows. Within these walls squalling infants had had their first—and aged grandparents their last—glimpse of this world. In these rooms people had loved, had known happiness and sorrow, and no doubt a fair amount of anger, jealousy, and frustration. The house had sheltered them all, and now it was sheltering me and mine. I felt that we were a part of its history, too.

Someone had set out a slightly crooked row of pine trees west of the house and they must have been fifty or sixty years old. They had no branches at all on the first fifteen feet of their trunks, but they had grown very tall and reached above the house. Sometimes the wind seemed to caress these trees with a heavenly hand, making their branches resonate like the strings of a harp. "Hush," I would tell my noisy children at such times. "Be quiet and listen to the harp in the trees," for I wanted them to hear the song of the pines, too. Alas, I was the only one who ever heard it.

A pair of orioles returned year after year to build their nest in one of the pines. Firmly woven of grass and bits of binder twine, the nest hung like a small bag about twenty feet above the ground. We saw the bright orange and black male often, for he never ventured very far from his favorite tree. But we never saw the female enter or leave her nest, nor did we ever see any of the fledglings come off the nest or learn to fly. It was maddening to think that the orioles had raised their families virtually under our noses and we had missed all these important events.

The female was especially shy and I had a good look at her only once. I happened to be standing at the kitchen door, idly waiting for William to come in for lunch, when that lovely, olive green creature flew down and sat on the sidewalk only a few feet away. I stood motionless, almost in awe of her. She scanned the sidewalk but could find no bugs or beetles there. Then she saw me—too big, too strange, too threatening—and she flew away. It was hard to see how a creature so small could migrate hundreds of miles, find her familiar nesting place, lay eggs, hatch little ones, and find enough food to feed them and herself.

Six weeks after we moved to the old house at the end of the lane our third son was born. If, as several people suggested, it was too bad that we hadn't had a daughter, I was quick to point out that I was very pleased with Jimmy. Anyway, what was wrong with having three boys in a row? As far as I was concerned—nothing!

I had spent the months before Jimmy's arrival worrying— needlessly, as it turned out. But how was I to know that? I was so relieved that the both of us were alive that I came back to the old house and my now much heavier burden of work with a happy heart.

Childbirth can be a very difficult time for a woman, but I believe that today's women are less inclined to worry about it than previous generations have been. William was not a worrier so I had kept my dreary premonitions about dying to myself, both before and after Jimmy was born. I thought it best not to say anything because I was afraid William would give me that old women-have-babies-every-day line and that would have demeaned the whole process for womankind in general and me in particular.

I had always wanted a family, always wanted to share in what is euphemistically known as "woman's supreme experience." But I had had that experience three times now, and I certainly could have done with something a little less supreme. I liked my mother's philosophy about childbirth which, no doubt, had been passed down to her from Evalina, that wise and redoubtable mother of eleven and midwife to many others. "It's too bad that the man can't have every other baby," my mother used to tell me whenever the subject came up. "The woman, understandably, would have the first one, then it would be the husband's turn. He would never have more than one. So that would end the baby business right there."

My mother was always fond of telling what happened when I was born. Her doctor had been very concerned about her, which was why he had asked another doctor to assist him. Both were horse and buggy doctors—the only kind we had in those days.

Now that first doctor was my parents' favorite, their standby in times of trouble. He was efficient and kind and he came no matter what the weather. Besides, he drove a big, long-legged gelding that could take him the twelve miles to our house in a hurry. He was our number one doctor and Mother always liked to tell how he had "pulled us through" one thing or another.

But that second doctor was something else again. He drove a lumpy old mare named Hazel, and she wasn't in any hurry to get anywhere. Number Two was an alcoholic and he always took his bottle along to tide him over the wearying miles while he made his calls in the country. Consequently, he had a disturbing propensity for getting lost. This made it hard for Hazel, who walked and walked and got very tired. She would often pull into a farmyard—any old farmyard—in the hope that it was the right one. Sometimes it was, sometimes it wasn't. If it was, then the doctor would attend his patient. If it wasn't then he turned Hazel around and got her out on the road again. Number Two would often arrive at his patient's bedside besotted to within the last inch of his Hippocratic oath. But no matter. Some people thought he was a better doctor drunk than other doctors were sober.

However, we never had a chance to find out the night that I was born. Number One got there first and he took care of everything.

Number Two didn't even show up. But he did stop at a farmhouse to telephone our doctor and explain that he had gotten lost.

"Hell! You can get lost again!" Number One shouted into the telephone. "It's all over now. The baby is here."

Now there were five of us in the old house at the end of the lane. I had always said that I would have six children. But that was in my youth, when I didn't know what it was all about. I knew now—and I decided that three was enough.

I have always admired women who have raised a dozen children or more. Even five or six is a respectable number to have. But I marvel at the mothers of really large families like twelve or fourteen. Where do these women find the strength and the patience?

And the strange part of it is that these women often look younger at forty than their counterparts who have borne only one or two children. I used to ask myself—how could this be? After giving it much thought, I came to a decision. The reason these women looked so young was because they didn't worry about getting pregnant all the time.

Starting from Scratch

THINGS are so different now. Very few farm women raise chickens anymore. It is such a simple matter to buy a dressed fryer or a dozen eggs at the supermarket. But there was a time when all farm women raised chickens. I don't think we ever made much money on them. Yet it was awfully nice to have all the fryers our families could eat. A fat, young hen roasted with her gravy served over mashed potatoes or hot biscuits was filling and delicious. Or you could boil the hen and cook noodles or dumplings in her rich broth.

We never ate a hen unless she was a good layer, bright of eye and red of comb. Sometimes she would have a half-formed egg in her and the yolk would be firm and golden. I always cooked it in the same pot with the hen and brought it to the table nestled close beside her on the same platter. I would feel some compunction then, at the sight of that round, yellow fruit of her femaleness.

"If we hadn't killed her she would have laid an egg today," I would say, somewhat sadly.

I always felt protective of my hens. They were such gentle birds and they went around happily scratching in the straw most of the day. They were so earnest about sitting on their nests to lay their eggs. When one of them succeeded in expelling her egg, she would look at it and maybe touch it with her beak as if she was a little surprised at having accomplished such a fine feat. Then she would fly off the nest cackling and that would make all the other hens cackle. I could hear them at the house and the sound was as music to my ears.

I was downright fond of my hens, but I had no kindly feelings toward the roosters. They usually got mean as soon as they reached maturity and they had long spurs on their legs, which they were ready to use at the slightest provocation. Roosters were something you fried when they were young and tender and crated up and sold when they got older. However, we always kept a few for our Thanksgiving and Christmas dinners. Turkeys were not as available then and, besides, the roosters didn't cost us anything.

We farm women took our chicken raising seriously, no doubt because the proceeds from this operation were generally conceded to be women's money, to be used as we saw fit. And we all started from scratch, you might say.

My work began in the spring when we brought the little birds home as innocent, helpless balls of fluff, and it continued throughout their growing period—right up to the time when the roosters were sold and the pullets were housed as layers in the fall. During these months I did all the work, although William helped care for the laying hens in the winter. But this was all right because I really didn't want him to help me very often. The chickens were mine and I was proud of them and wanted to take care of them myself.

But ah! There was many a slip 'twixt chick and lip, as I was to discover. Nobody could help loving a baby chick scarcely out of its shell—a chick so tiny and soft. Holding one in my hand with his beady eyes so trusting, his body warm and caressable, brought out my deepest maternal instincts. Here was a helpless infant, fully dependent on me, and I vowed to give him every chance for life that I could. This was the way I started out every spring.

But my euphoria was soon displaced by grim reality. The chicks grew rapidly and by the fourth or fifth day they weren't lovable anymore. The delightful, fuzzy look of infancy was gone and their coarse wing feathers were coming in. They were fast approaching the gawky stage.

By the time they had been out of their shells two weeks, the chicks were absorbing germs like a blotter. And if disease didn't kill them they looked around for ways to commit suicide. One of their favorite diseases was pneumonia, to which they would succumb very quickly and in large numbers. Another disease was coccidiosis, which made their heads and wings hang down and pasted them up behind in a most disgusting fashion. They hunted the corners of the brooder house assiduously in search of small specks of poisonous mold and they delighted in finding a bit of string large enough to choke on. They drowned themselves in their waterers and allowed themselves to be trampled to death by their fellow chicks.

Their favorite game was something called "cannibalism." By the time a chick was two or three weeks old he had discovered that he had a sharp beak and that it was fun to peck one of his inoffensive siblings. One peck drew blood. The blood tasted good to him and soon he was chasing his quarry with a vengeance. Other chicks were attracted to the bright red blood and soon they, too, were pecking the hapless bird. If you weren't right there to rescue him he would die very quickly. Their appetites whetted, the little cannibals would then be off working on another victim. You could buy stuff to put in the water which was supposed to stop this sort of thing, but often it did no good. Once a cannibal always a cannibal.

I had struggled along for years with a kerosene brooder stove that heated the whole brooder house. But it gave off awful fumes, was always running out of kerosene, and we were afraid it would catch the building on fire. One day a salesman came along and talked me into buying an electric brooder. This stayed warm under its canopy but left the brooder house itself unheated. "An electric brooder is every bit as good as a mother hen," the salesman told me. "The chicks learn right away where the source of heat is. They will come out from under the canopy to eat and drink. But if they get cold they will run back under the canopy."

It sounded great and I could hardly wait to get another batch of chicks. I was so enthused over the new brooder that I unwittingly bragged to Bee Bagley about it. "You'll be sorry," she warned. "Your chicks will come out from under the canopy and get chilled. Then they'll get pneumonia and die."

"But the salesman said they'd soon learn where the heat was. He said an electric brooder is every bit as good as an old hen," I argued.

"There isn't anything better than an old hen," Bee said. "An old hen is nature's way and you can't improve on nature.

That's the trouble with these salesmen. They're always running around pulling the wool over the eyes of people who are too dumb to know any better. Besides, what will you do when the electricity goes off? It will get so cold in your brooder house that your chicks will freeze to death."

"But the electricity doesn't go off very often," I said lamely. "And if it does I can keep the area under the canopy warm by putting jugs of hot water under it."

"Humph!" Bee snorted. "I can just see you chasing out there at two in the morning with jugs of hot water. That's too much work for me, and I like work!"

Bee was right about the brooder, although I would have died before I admitted it to her. My chicks came in mid-April that year, as lively a bunch of birds as I'd ever seen. But we had a cold spring and some snow fell as late as May. The electricity went off three times and I had plenty of chances to test the jugs-of-hot-water-under-the-canopy theory. It didn't work. A lot of the chicks got pneumonia and died and I thought I was going to get pneumonia myself from having to run out in the rain and cold to take care of them.

All chickens like to go to bed as soon as it gets dark. A mature chicken has sense enough to hie himself to the nearest roost shortly after the sun goes down. But young chickens can't fly to a roost. All they want to do is get into a dark corner, the trouble being that they all want to get into the same corner, and they just keep piling up on one another. Naturally, the ones on the bottom are likely to smother.

To avoid such a debacle, you are supposed to turn the lights on before it gets dark. But I was never very good at avoiding debacles and sometimes forgot the lights. When I remembered what I was supposed to do, I would race madly to the brooder house, my heart pounding at the sounds of chicken panic within. Sure enough, there would be at least one corner filled with terrified chickens, each one clawing at his fellows in a frantic effort to find a dark place to sleep.

This happened so many times that I finally developed my own system of artificial respiration. I would grab the top layers of birds and throw them aside, digging down to the bottom as quickly as I could. A few birds were apt to be dead, but there were others that were still breathing—although not much. I would grab a half-dead bird with both hands around his body, press his breast in and release it rhythmically, all the while calling him back from the grave with loud cries of, "Here chick! Here chick!" Sometimes it worked. The unconscious bird would start to breathe again and I would quickly toss him aside, grab another bird and repeat the process. I could usually save three or four this way, but if the birds had been piled up too long there was sure to be one or two dead ones.

It was rather nice to know that I could give artificial respiration to a chicken, but I never told anybody about it because, after all, whose fault was it that the birds had gotten piled up in the corner that way?

It was the same with your laying hens. You didn't crow unless you had something to crow about. If your hens were up to seventy percent production, you told it on the telephone so the news would get around. But if they were limping along at thirty percent production, you didn't mention it.

After the young birds learned to roost, most of my troubles were over. It wasn't long before they developed into fine chickens almost ready to eat. Each day I caught and examined a couple of them, feeling their legs like the old witch in Hansel and Gretel to see if they were large enough to fry. William refused to eat anything except the breasts, and the boys preferred the legs and thighs. This left all the scrawny necks, backs, gizzards, and livers for me. However, a few meals of fried chicken would make me decide that all those trips to the brooder house had been well worth it.

Our henhouse was the worst building on the farm, a dilapidated thing that hadn't seen a paint brush for thirty years. It leaned perilously, and how it ever withstood the wind I was never able to figure out. Its roof leaked and in the winter snow would blow in through the cracks. I asked the landlord if he would build a new henhouse and, while he thought it was a good idea, he didn't think it was so good that he wanted to do it. So we fixed the henhouse as best we could, nailing old boards or tin over the cracks and pounding stakes into the ground wherever there was a hole big enough to admit a snake or a raccoon. After we had made some repairs we would go inside to see how effective we had been. If we could still see daylight through the cracks we went back to work again.

With a henhouse like this, we had to have heavy hens that would withstand the cold, like Rhode Island Reds, or Buff Orpingtons, or Jersey Giants. The bigger the hen the more body heat she had and the more likely she was to lay well during the winter. Well do I remember the Jersey Giant hens. They laid eggs no matter how cold it got. I would go into the henhouse to find them sitting stoically on their nests, determined to lay even though the snow might be sifting in on their backs.

Although I detested carrying feed and water to the chickens, I enjoyed seeing them lined up at their feeders and waterers, red-combed heads bobbing up and down as they ate and drank. Lugging a bale of bedding to the henhouse was hard work but I had my reward when I saw with what satisfaction they capered around on the golden straw — scratching in it for the few oat kernels it might contain and clucking their pleasure at being warm and comfortable. At such times I would turn the feed pail upside down and sit there for a few minutes, the better to admire my feathered brood.

Ordinary roosters did not bring much money when they were sold in the fall. But capons were worth more and it was with this idea in mind that I learned to do surgical caponizing. I never killed a bird nor did I ever have a one testicle bird, which was known as a "slip." But I had to force myself to do the operations. Although I was assured that the birds felt almost no pain, they squawked constantly from start to finish. That squawking finally got to me. I was no sadist. After I roasted one capon and found that the meat was not much better than that of an ordinary chicken, I deprived no more males of their roosterhood.

I had many chances to caponize for the neighborhood women. Not that they would do such a terrible thing themselves, I was given to understand, but they would like to have a few capons to roast. I declined all requests. But I was rather proud of being able to caponize. It sort of took the sting out of not being able to milk a cow.

The capons became slow, docile birds that walked with a kind of flat-footed gait to enable them to support their weight, which could reach ten or twelve pounds. They were mild tempered and never fought. But there was no docility about roosters who were allowed to keep their maleness intact. They became proud, hot-tempered, and disdainful of all humans. Granted the privilege of spending the winter shut up with the hens they knew only two things—guard that harem with unwavering vigilance and mate with any hen that would allow it.

Elmer was a case in point. It was impossible to tell what breed of chicken he was. His under body was black but his back was brown. He had some blue-green and some dark red feathers on his head and those on his wing tips were a lovely emerald green. Elmer was quite a bird. He must have been a hybrid, chosen willy-nilly at the hatchery to fill out the required one hundred in a box of chicks.

The reason Elmer got to spend the winter in the henhouse was because he was too small to sell with the other roosters. So he, along with two other males, was housed with the hens that winter. And Elmer made the most of it. What he lacked in size he made up for in ferocity and soon he had the other roosters cowed. He watched the hens jealously, ready to pounce at the first sign of female interest. If, by chance, one of the other roosters could convince a hen to receive him, the act had to be performed surreptitiously in a dark corner of the henhouse. When it was done and Elmer had discovered that the passionate pair had put one over on him, his neck feathers would bristle with anger. Like a flash he was off to punish the luckless couple, chasing the unfaithful hen away before she scarcely had time to shake her feathers back in place and sailing into the other rooster with beak and claw. Elmer was mad about one thing or another all the time and we noticed that the whites of his eyes had turned blood red.

As winter wore on, Elmer added me to his enemies' list. I was watched with a baleful eye from the time I came in the henhouse until I left. He invariably made a rush toward me as I opened the door to leave. When I turned to face him he would stop his charge and stand still with a don't-look-at-me-I-didn't-do-anything expression. Day by day, he became braver. I tried never to turn my back on him but that didn't help much because he sneaked up on me anyway.

One day as I was pouring feed into a trough, I heard the sudden whir of wings behind me and found that I had long, bloody scratches from thigh to ankle. "Something has to be done with Elmer," I told William that night, exhibiting my scratches. "He's always sneaking up behind me and it's getting so I dread going into the henhouse."

"What do you want me to do with him? Shoot him?" William inquired.

"No, don't shoot him. I believe I'll butcher him and make some noodles. He's probably too tough to roast and I'm sure he won't be very big. But he ought to make a nice kettle of noodles," I said.

So it was agreed. Elmer would die. William went up that night, plucked the rooster off the roost, decapitated him, pulled his feathers off, and brought him to the house for me to dress. "Elmer was much bigger than I thought he'd be. Look how nice and plump he is," I said later, displaying the white, unoffending carcass as I put it into the refrigerator to chill.

Elmer would indeed make a fine pot of noodles. I put him on to cook early the next morning and then went to the henhouse to tend the other birds. I approached my chores without trepidation, thinking that my old enemy was dead. But as soon as I opened the door I realized that William, having had only a flashlight to assist him, had gotten the wrong rooster. There Elmer stood, pulled up to his full height, chest thrust out in Napoleonic pride. His red eyes were glaring at me as hatefully as ever.

In the spring we turned the hens out and Elmer with them. The hens, glad to be released from their winter's prison, scratched happily for worms and bugs, going back to the henhouse only when the urge to lay their eggs came upon them. Elmer tended his harem with what seemed at times to be a touching solicitude. If he found a tasty morsel — a particularly large beetle, for instance, or a kernel of corn or an oat that had a tempting sprout on it — he would not eat it himself but would cluck invitingly to the hens to come and get it. No doubt he was hoping that this husbandly concern would pay off in the long run, for now that the hens were outdoors he had a lot more running to do.

Sometimes a hen would refuse to squat after he had done his courtship dance around her. With typical femaleness, she would play hard to get, racing coquettishly around the corncrib or the barn or even across the road, all the while squawking loud protestations of unwillingness as Elmer chased after her in hot pursuit. Occasionally, a hen would win the race and Elmer would drop out in disgust. But usually he stayed on her trail until she conceded defeat and allowed him to have his way.

I suppose Elmer was defending his territory the day he got into a fight with the tractor. He had a lot of ground to defend now and he was determined to see that every square foot of it was reserved for him and his harem. William had brought Gertrude in to plow the garden that day and the chickens were running here and there, searching in the upturned soil for bugs and worms. Elmer happened to get in Gertrude's path and he refused to give ground as she approached. The closer she came the madder he got. His neck feathers stiffened and he flapped his wings and charged. Twice he did this—and backed off within inches of that big wheel. But Gertrude just kept coming and once again Elmer sailed into her. This time he didn't get away fast enough and we saw him go under the wheel, a crumpled mass of feathers. As soon as the wheel passed over him he scrambled to his feet and shook himself in disbelief. He was somewhat chastened, to be sure, but he was alive and unhurt. The soft ground had cushioned his body and saved him from what might well be called a "crushing" defeat.

Having a run-in with Gertrude didn't teach Elmer a thing. In fact, we thought it increased his hatred for us. If he saw any of us coming he made ferocious attacks, jumping off the ground a couple of feet and lashing out at us with his razor-sharp claws. One day I sent son Bill to the henhouse for some eggs and he ran back a few minutes later, blood flowing from a long gash in his cheek. It wasn't a deep cut, but it had come perilously close to his left eye. Elmer had been hiding in a corner, Bill said, and had attacked him before he realized he was there.

William had had enough. "That damned rooster," he said angrily as he went for his shotgun. "I'll fix him! I should have killed him a long time ago." He strode out the door and a few minutes later we heard a single blast from the gun. Elmer's defiance in his hour of execution was reminiscent of a brave spy facing the rifle squad. He made it easy for William. He stood his ground and stuck out his chest and made himself a perfect target.

We never did figure out what made Elmer so mean. Maybe

it was because he had started life as a runt and had to fight his way to maturity. Maybe he just had an oversupply of roosterish hormones, or maybe some of his ancestors had been fighting cocks. Nor did we ever know why the whites in his eyes had turned red, but I surmised that he had worked himself into a tizzy so many times he had simply broken all his blood vessels.

At any rate, we never did have any other red-eyed roosters, nor did we ever have another one that equaled Elmer in pugnacity. He was a hot-tempered, undersized, oversexed people-hater, and the best your could say for him was that he had pretty feathers.

"If You'll Do the Work"

M OST landlords are not very keen on spending their money. What funds they invest in fixing up a farm are small and usually doled out a little at a time. And if a renter wants to get along with his landlord he has to understand this. The renter also knows that he can facilitate matters by doing the work himself.

"If you'll do the work yourself." That was a line we would hear many times. "I'll buy the shingles if you'll fix the roof." "I'll buy the planks if you'll build the bridge." "I'll buy the wallpaper if you'll put it on."

I can't say that we ever became accomplished do-it-your-selvers, but we tried. One of the things we learned to do, although not very well, was hang wallpaper. We would begin early in the morning. I would make a big kettle of paste by pouring boiling water into a lot of cornstarch. William measured off the number of feet of paper we needed. But I was the official *cutter-offer* and *paste slapper-oner*.

We never found a straight corner in the old house. A strip of paper always had to be overlapped at the top to make it cover the wall at the bottom, or vice versa. It took both of us to guide the paper into place and if it didn't cover where it was supposed to we had to peel it off and start over again. Both dining and living rooms were large; the dining room was sixteen feet long and putting on a strip of ceiling paper was not a job for the faint hearted.

I remember the first strip of paper we ever put on that long ceiling. I was dubious about it, but William didn't seem to be

too concerned; he was still smoking his cigar. He had two step-
ladders spaced several feet apart, with a plank laid between
them to walk on. While I slapped the paste on, he eyed the
ceiling so he'd know exactly how the paper should be put on, he
told me.

He took one end of the paper and I took the other. He
climbed up on the stepladder, stuck the paper to the ceiling,
spread it down the middle with his brush, and walked along the
plank. So far, things were looking good, I told him.

But they weren't good at all. The paper had suddenly
veered toward the northeast and it lacked a good two inches of
covering the ceiling at one end. There was only one thing to do.

A do-it-yourself job

We had to peel it off again. Now this peeling off thing was something you had to watch. The paper was cheap and not very strong. When it was wet it would tear easily. William was aware now that we had gotten ourselves into a real bind and on his second attempt he supported the paper on the top of his head. It was too much. The paper split and William's head, cigar and all, emerged through the hole.

We could paper a room in a day, but there was paste over everything, including us, when we were done. I hated wallpapering with a vengeance. But William was good natured about it all and stopped working only long enough to light his cigar.

William and I were diametrically opposed when it came to work. I gave work a great deal of thought and often worried over what had to be done, while he just got busy and did it. I guess the reason was that he liked hard work—an admirable quality, to be sure. But I often wished he wasn't so damned cheerful about it.

He took everything calmly, while I was quite apt to blow a fuse over something that he didn't even consider important. I chattered a lot but I fear he didn't even listen to me part of the time. He never said a cross word to me. But what was worse—he often said no words at all. I think it would have done both of us good if we had had a rousing quarrel every now and then. And I was perfectly willing. But he wasn't. I suppose this kind of domestic tranquility was good for the boys when they were growing up. However, their father must have seemed very gentle and mild-mannered to them, while I must have come across as a hot-tempered, irascible harridan, a mother who was always complaining about something. I am older now and I have learned to accept life with more equanimity. But I fear that I did more than my share of what is sometimes rather inelegantly known as "bitching" in those days.

The trouble was that William had patience and I didn't. He always told me that I could learn patience if I tried. But I always thought patience was something you were born with, like big ankle bones, or a tendency to gain weight even if you walked by the stove and sniffed the stew while it was cooking. So I didn't try to change myself. I figured I was the same now as I was that night when Number One had gotten mad at Number Two and told him to get lost.

But William was different. He possessed the fine and estimable characteristic of patience in vast quantities. William was patient with wallpapering, carrying laundry water, landlords, unpatched overalls, lost hammers, corn husking, broken fences, kids, lost pliers, holes in his socks, dogs that snarled, fourteen-hour workdays—and neighbors.

One time Pete Neumann called at nine o'clock at night and told William that his bull had gotten himself down in a thirty-foot ravine with steep sides and would William please bring his lantern and come and help him get the creature out? Pete apologized to William when he got there. "I hated to ask you," he said. "But I knew you were the only man in the neighborhood who would help get a bull out of a ditch in the dark."

The do-it-yourself jobs, therefore, posed no problems for William, who approached all of them with the same, unruffled it-has-to-be-done-so-let's-do-it philosophy. He even built a bridge by himself. We had a bridge that spanned a small creek adjacent to the pasture. I say the creek was "small" because it didn't have much water in it. It was fed by a spring that sometimes ran and sometimes didn't. But that mere trickle of water over the last hundred years or so had managed to cut deep into the ground, so now there was a twenty-foot ravine with that little ribbon of water at the bottom. The cows had to cross this bridge to and from their way to pasture. The stringers under the bridge had once been set solidly into the creek banks, but rains had washed the soil out from under them and they were teetering perilously. The whole thing was on the verge of falling into the creek and possibly taking a few cows along with it. So William told the landlord about it. He got a familiar answer. "I'll buy the stringers and planks if you'll do the work."

The landlord, true to his word, sent a truck out with some old railroad ties to be used as stringers and heavy planks to serve as flooring. William had never built a bridge before but he knew how it ought to be done, and he started one morning as soon as the cows had been taken across the old bridge to pasture. First, he hooked Gertrude's drawbar to the stringers and pulled the old bridge loose. Anything that fell into the creek was allowed to stay there, but what came up on the bank was piled up to use as firewood. Then he cut deeper moorings farther back into the banks on both sides of the creek to hold the new stringers, which were much stronger than the old ones had been. Now all he had left to do was lay the planks on one by one and nail them securely to the stringers.

By prodigious effort, he managed to get the bridge built in less than a day and he finished just in time, for the cows had to be brought in soon for their evening milking. William was tired. He had worked all day but he was proud of his accomplishment.

"Don't you want to look at the bridge?" he asked me later that afternoon.

I detected a wistfulness in his voice, a desire to have his first do-it-yourself bridge appraised and approved, and so I went. I jumped on the bridge and noticed that it didn't shake like the old one had.

"You built a real nice bridge," I told him. "It's good and solid. You must have saved the landlord a lot of money today."

William beamed with pride. "This ought to keep the cows from falling into the creek," he said.

And so it would have. But we thought for a while that the cows were never going to set foot on the bridge. William rounded them up from the pasture and brought them down to it. They stopped a few feet from the bridge and just stood there, wide eyed and suspicious. We got behind them and urged them to cross but they refused to budge

William thought they might be alarmed by the two older boys who were running back and forth across the bridge. So we banished them to the car with small Jimmy. It was quieter now but the cows remained unconvinced. William decided it was time he asserted his authority and he picked up a stick and whacked a couple of bovine backsides. The offended cows were startled but adamant. Cross that bridge they would not.

"Why don't you let them rest a while?" I suggested. "Maybe when they've had time to examine the bridge they'll decide to go across." But this didn't help, either. The pressure being off, some of the cows remembered their cuds and they brought them up and chewed thoughtfully, cautious eyes always on the bridge. William soon saw that this ploy would not work. "They'll be here all night at this rate," he said.

I heard Jimmy crying and I turned to walk across the bridge, calling "So bos, so bos" to the cows. That did it. All that they had been waiting for was proof that the bridge was safe for them to walk on. To the last cow, they followed me meekly across. What was good enough for me was good enough for them, they must have thought.

Or do cows think? We'll probably never know. Vain and proud as we humans are, we like to believe that we are the only ones capable of thinking. Yet that day we had seen supposedly "dumb" animals give what appeared to be a reasoned response to what must have looked to them as a threatening situation. Ordinary, phlegmatic, cud-chewing milk cows they were, their kind condemned forever to serving man with their milk and their meat—not even allowed to reproduce except for profit. But after I had seen them wait until that do-it-yourself bridge had been proven safe I was less inclined to look upon them as dumb animals.

Cows actually baby-sit for one another. During the grazing season, one cow will lie down in the pasture with her own calf nearby and several other calves gathered around her. While this cow baby-sits, the other cows are free to graze where they will— serene in the knowledge that their offspring are being guarded. This is a common and always heartwarming sight, surely one that shows not only deep maternal instincts but also some degree of intelligence. How do the cows decide which one will baby-sit and which ones will graze? I was never able to figure that out.

Besides the wallpapering and the bridge building there were a lot of other do-it-yourself jobs on the farm. I bandaged old walls to keep the plaster from falling off, applied numerous coats of paint to scarred woodwork, and occasionally puttied in a loose window. William patched roofs, repaired barn doors, filled ditches, cleared brush, mowed weeds, and fixed pumps and windmills.

Fence repair was a job that a tenant farmer was expected to do himself, of course. Our landlords would occasionally buy a roll of new barbed wire. But usually a section of weak fencing was repaired with used barbed wire, mainly because we had that on hand, and it was easier and more diplomatic to use it than it was to ask the landlord for new. Besides, there was no time to waste. If the cows were out of the pasture you had to get them back in again. The trick was to keep them there.

It seemed to me that William was continually fixing fences. He used a wire stretcher to pull the fence tight and the old wire would frequently break, bound back, and cut him. He shrugged these minor wounds off, but there was so much fence repairing to be done that he was seldom without scratches on his forearms.

Trees have the unhappy faculty for growing where they aren't wanted. This was true of the nine big trees along the road leading to the house at the end of the lane. Those old elms would have to come out, the landlord told us one day, although he didn't say exactly how or when this was to be done.

However, this seemed like another one of those do-it-yourself jobs, and one for which we were admirably suited because we had a long cross-cut saw that was designed for two people. All we would have to do was use that saw and a little elbow grease, William told me, and we'd have those trees down in no time. He grabbed the handle on one end of the saw and I grabbed the other. I pushed when William pulled. He pushed when I pulled. Back and forth we went, hour after hour. The job required three days, but we were quite proud of ourselves when we had the trees trimmed, the brush hauled off, and the limbs and trunks piled up to be cut into firewood later.

We could hardly wait for the landlord to see what we had done. But when he came out his reaction was something less than heartwarming.

"What did you do it for?" he asked. "I intended to hire a bulldozer to take those trees out."

It would have been nice if he had given us the money that he would otherwise have spent on the bulldozing. But he didn't.

"Well, no matter," William told me later. "Our intentions were good. We just jumped into the collar too soon."

Observations from the Distaff Side

I'M sure it never occurred to any of us farm women to go out in the world and "do our own thing." Besides, we were already doing our own thing, which usually consisted of doing what was expected of us. And this was the way we had been brought up. The rationale was simple in those days. A girl would get married some day—right? Therefore, it was necessary for her to learn the "womanly" arts of housekeeping and cooking. Those were the days when nobody had heard of the ERA, and women's lib was no more than a gleam in somebody's eye.

Nevertheless, there was a great deal of ambiguity in the advice my mother gave me. She never told me that housekeeping might drive me up the wall, and I didn't know how hard I'd have to try before I became a credible cook.

However, I started my married life with the best of intentions. I told myself that I would be an exemplary wife. I had been brought up to think that the way to a man's heart is through his stomach, and I made up my mind that I would cook everything my new husband wanted exactly the way he wanted it. I set out on this rocky road to culinary excellence long before I was married. Yet I discovered as soon as I got out of my mother's kitchen and into my own that I knew a lot less than I thought I did.

But I was willing, and I tried to dig myself out of this pit of incompetency with a measuring cup and a teaspoon. Poor William! There must have been times when he wished he could trade me in on a different model—somebody who resembled a child bride a lot less and his mother a lot more.

One of our earliest problems turned out to be simply a matter of semantics. Once, before we were married, he asked me how I was on making cakes. I assumed he meant chocolate or angelfood or spice cakes. So I practically knocked myself out learning to bake CAKE cakes. Several weeks after we were married I found out that he didn't mean these at all. What he meant was griddle cakes, the kind a hard-working man likes for breakfast.

He suggested that I ask his mother how to make griddle cakes, and I did. But somehow her recipe got garbled in the translation and I used two cups of flour when I should have used one. Her pancakes were light as a cloud, while mine strongly resembled a piece of plywood. I went back to her for further instructions and finally managed to come up with something edible. But I thought baking griddle cakes was a lot of work, and it did my ego no good when William told me that his mother had made pancakes almost every morning for a family of eight and had thought nothing of it.

Slowly but surely over the years, it dawned on me that William and I were not on the same wave length when it came to food.

What William liked, he really liked, as I discovered early on. If I asked him on a morning of our first year of married life what he wanted for dinner that night I always got the same answer—breaded pork chops and apple pie. Consistent with my desire to be a perfect wife, I got busy and fulfilled those requests. But after the first twelve months I rebelled and said I'd never bread another pork chop or make another apple pie as long as I lived. I suppose this must have been the point at which he realized the honeymoon was over.

One of William's great loves was baking powder biscuits, which I thought were dry and tasteless, and he thought were simply delicious. Nevertheless, it was apparent that baking powder biscuits were something William had to have to keep his whole life from going down the drain. But I considered them a terrible nuisance and didn't make them except for rare occasions—usually when I wanted something. He used to butter me up by telling me that I made the best damned biscuits in the country. But this blandishment didn't do him much good. I simply accepted the plaudit and avoided the biscuit making as long as I could. I found all sorts of things to complain about. Biscuits were such messy things to make, I would tell him. And it took two basketfuls of cobs to get the stove roiled up to the point where they would brown in the oven. I got so I was pretty good at reading the signs. If William began to look wistful and talked about the good old days when his mother had been doing the cooking, then I knew it was time to get busy. But I was sporadic at best about the biscuit chores. I waited until I thought he had reached the limit of his endurance or until the spirit moved me—whichever came first.

And William let me get away with this. I didn't realize how lucky I was until we were neighbors to a two-generation household and I found out that the aged mother had gotten up early every day of her life to bake breakfast biscuits for her fortyish son. When she died the daughter-in-law took up where the mother had left off. The day I heard that story I came home feeling very grateful for my long-suffering husband.

William was no complainer. He simply didn't eat anything he didn't want to eat. Although it was obvious that he enjoyed some foods more than others, he very seldom asked me to prepare any specific food. Maybe he was afraid he would start the whole breaded-pork-chop-apple-pie syndrome all over again.

My mother was an excellent cook, and I tried to emulate her. She had always made what I thought was superb fruit salad. She mixed several kinds of fruits and you got a lot of pineapple and cherries and white grapes in her salad. She went easy on the banana because it had a tendency to turn black and she didn't like that. She put this salad in fancy sherbet dishes and served it with whipped cream and a sprinkling of walnuts on top. It was a dessert we had often for company dinners, when it was served with cake, and also for the family when we were eating alone. So I wanted to keep up my mother's tradition.

William was polite about this fruit salad and I suppose we must have been married ten years before I found out how he really felt about it. He came home from haying at Neumanns' one day and spoke glowingly of Henrietta's dinner. I inquired as to what she had and he named off all the usual things—meat, potatoes, gravy.

"She sure had some good jello," he said.

"What did she have in it?" I asked.

"Bananas," he answered.

Then I knew.

I always baked beans, starting from scratch with the dry ones and sometimes prepared them with fresh pork, other times using tomato juice, onion, and bacon. Either way required several hours of almost constant attendance and much stoking of Devil or Satan to bring them to the proper stage of doneness. This was something else my mother had taught me how to do. She, in turn, had learned it from my father's mother. So the bean baking was another family tradition I carried on. I was inordinately proud of my homemade beans. Baking them was one of the few things that set me apart from the other farm women. They were my only claim to fame. Let's face it. I was downright jealous over my beans and I didn't want anybody else to bake any like them.

I knew that William liked my beans, for he ate vast quantities of them whenever I fixed them. But I sometimes wondered if they were worth the effort. Occasionally, he would come home from a haying or a threshing job and tell me that Bee, or Henrietta, or Lolly Nelson had had some really good beans for dinner. To me, of course, that was just like waving a red flag in front of a bull, and I would call that woman up the very next day and ask her how she fixed her beans.

The usual answer was, "I bought a gallon of Van Camp's, put some sugar in them, laid a few strips of bacon on top, and baked them an hour."

That was it. She hadn't put the beans to soak overnight, hadn't carried a lot of fuel to bake them for eight hours, hadn't peeked in on them every thirty minutes while they baked.

Of course, that other woman, whoever she was, was the smart one. She hadn't gone to all that work and I didn't need to, either. But I had a motive behind my madness. I was trying to create a reputation for myself as the neighborhood bean baker. I couldn't milk a cow. I had to do something.

William liked his chicken young and fried to a crisp. He ate only the breast meat, however, and preferred the end with the wishbone. He ate the dumplings or noodles when I cooked a hen. But he refused to eat the hen.

He was suspicious of home-canned meat too. He was afraid

we would all get poisoned on it, he said. I assured him it was perfectly all right, that my mother had always canned meat at home and none of us had died from eating it. However, he would eat the gravy off of this meat. I used to quote him the old adage that one might as well eat the devil as drink his broth. But he remained unconvinced, and I made one batch of canned meat and that was all.

William wouldn't eat corn except from the cob, so I canned the ears whole. I would pack the stuff in gallon jars and process it in a hot water bath in the wash boiler for three hours. I was very proud of this corn. I could get seven or eight stubby ears in each jar, and it looked so appetizing sitting on the shelf in the root cellar when the snow was flying outside. I continued to can this corn until Bee warned me that it was dangerous to can a nonacid vegetable in such large containers. But I had flirted with ptomaine for three years before anybody told me about it.

My homemade bread, however, was something about which there was never any contention. We all ate that. I had grown up seeing my mother mix and knead bread and I thought I knew how it was done, so I started on this project soon after I was married. The first rolls I ever made glowered at me all day and refused to rise. I knew I had to do something with them so I baked them anyway. They came out of the oven as heavy as lead and as tough as shoe leather. But William ate them with relish and I persevered, anxious to please him. After many failures and near failures I got so I could bake huge loaves, fluffy on the inside and brown and crusty on the outside. During the years when the boys were young, I baked six loaves twice each week and usually topped this off with a pan of three dozen cinnamon rolls, baked while Satan was hot and still in the mood.

Commercially baked bread is as nothing—a mere whiff, with no body and no character. But a slice of homemade bread is chewy, filling, and satisfying. If you have homemade bread you can serve the simplest of foods with it and everything will taste great. Even the lowly sardine or a fried egg or a bowl of soup will make a delicious meal, if you have plenty of homemade bread to eat with it. I highly recommend bread baking to all young mothers. No child ought to be deprived of the joy of coming home from school and finding his mother's very own bread sitting on the cooling racks. That bread will become a pleasant memory that your children will carry with them always.

The art of bread baking—and it is an art—grows on one. My mother baked her own bread until she was almost ninety; my father was lucky enough to live out his whole life knowing no other kind of bread. She baked two loaves every Saturday and she was distressed when she no longer had the strength to mix it up and knead it.

"What I would give to be able to bake bread again," she would tell me wistfully.

When I would go to see her during those last years, I would often find her sitting on a chair in front of her stove, watching her bread, and turning it so it would get brown evenly on all sides. I used to tell her that she didn't have to do this with an electric stove, that all she had to do was set the temperature and walk away. But she would have none of this advice. She would watch that bread while it baked and that was that.

What Mother was doing, of course, was trying to come up with that perfect loaf of bread every time and, in so doing, she was trying to prove her worth as a cook and a woman. She had never held down a job outside her home. Her house was her life. This was all she knew and she was determined to have everything right. As a young girl, I had often resented the way she insisted on having a spotless house, on having clothes ironed and neatly placed in dresser drawers, on measuring out to the last teaspoonful everything that went into her baking. She was seeking perfection and she had fallen into a trap, I used to think.

But I'm afraid my generation, especially we farm women, fell into much the same trap. In those days, nobody tried to assure us of our worth as individuals. I think all of us women sensed this in one way or another. As wives and mothers, we knew we were important, of course. But our work was not confined to the home. We saw how hard our husbands worked and we yearned to help out. Many women assisted with the livestock chores or did some of the milking. A few even drove tractors and helped with the field work, and they still do.

The first time I ever saw Henrietta Neumann she was

standing up on a murderously toothed harrow, driving four horses, and making the dust fly when she crossed the field. I knew I could never do anything like that, but I admired her because she could. She had always lived on a farm and done field work all her life, the neighbors told me. So she'd never had to overcome the stigma of being a "town woman." But the fact that she could handle four horses set her apart from the rest of us.

We women were an extra pair of hands, an extra set of shoulders to share the burden. And it has alway been so with farm women. Grandmother Lightell had carried an apron full of seed corn to the field and dropped it into the little holes that Grandpa made with his hoe. I was doing much the same thing when I used a corn knife to chop ear corn into bite sized slices for the heifers. I suppose both Evalina and I were trying to prove that our husbands couldn't get along with us.

If you weren't afraid to round up the cows (I was) when they had broken into the alfalfa field—then you rounded up those cows. If you had the courage (I didn't) to step in among the brood sows and rescue a helpless baby pig after his mother had lain down on him and was slowly crushing him to death—then you rescued that pig. If a farmer had a wife who could do these sorts of things he could leave for the field in the morning without a worry in the world.

Still, our priorities lay with our families, our gardening, our chicken raising and canning. I fear we all tried to outdo ourselves and everybody else, too. If you had a culinary skill then you honed it and sharpened it until you had built yourself a reputation among the other women. If you could take four-teen egg whites and whip them into a delicate angelfood cake that stood eight inches high when you took it out of the oven—then you made those cakes and served them to the club women and hay men with pride. If you could raise big heads of snowy cauliflower when nobody else did—then you raised big heads of snowy cauliflower. And if you made the best damned beet pick-les in the country—then you got busy every summer and put up twenty quarts of the best damned beet pickles in the country.

That was the way we lived. Our work was hard and often boring. You had to get your satisfaction from knowing that it was creditably done. But oh! How I longed to leave it all behind sometimes. I yearned to chuck the work and make an unscheduled trip to town or to the neighbors. However, William and I did not see eye to eye on this. He thought my willingness to drop everything on the spur of the moment was positively juvenile. And I guess I was just trying to be a kid again. I remembered how it was when my parents lived on the farm. My father would have to go to town and Mother and Gladys and Don and I would go along. If Mother didn't have time to get us all gussied up she made us sit in the car. But at least we enjoyed the drive (a big deal in those days), and these trips usually ended with ice cream cones all around.

William, however, thought it was foolish to waste all that time. He would stick his head in the back door and yell, "I'm going to town. Be back in an hour or two." The reason he had to yell was because I wasn't within sight. It seemed to me that I was always busy making beds in the farthest corner of the house when he got these notions. But I could hear him, and I would yell, "Wait for me! I want to go, too!" Then I would race madly from the bedroom, through the living room, through the dining room and into the kitchen, kicking the toys out of the way as I went. I never succeeded in making it on time. When I reached the porch William would already have the car aimed for town.

If I expressed my disappointment when William got home, he would defend himself with waspishly sweet reasonableness. He had needed those nails or those staples immediately, he would tell me. He didn't have time to wait on a woman who always had to look through three drawers before she found a pair of runnerless hose. It made sense, didn't it? Of course it did.

Different people—different wave lengths.

I wasn't on the same wave length as the neighbor women when it came to housekeeping, either. They were all wonderful housekeepers. On a scale of one to ten there wasn't anybody who would have fallen below an eight. They went into spasms of activity every spring and fall and cleaned and straightened everything. They went after mud, soot, ashes, and lint with equal fervor. I always figured they had scared the hell out of their dust. Once they had it cleaned up it never had the nerve to show its face again.

This was in sharp contrast to me, however. It was hard to tell where my spring housecleaning left off and my fall cleaning began. There was never any clear-cut line of demarcation when everything in the house was all clean at the same time.

It would have been nice if someone had told us women how important we were and what fine contributions we were making in those days. But nobody did. So we just did the work and kept quiet about it, pulling ourselves up by our own emotional bootstraps if that became necessary.

Ah! Where was women's lib when we needed it?

Timber, Meadow, and Muriel

THE landlord continued to make modest improvements on the place, although we went without electricity for three years after we moved there. But he paid for the wiring gladly when the power line came our way. We lived there for five or six years before he painted the house on the outside. Then he told us that was all he would do to the house for many years. I gathered that he didn't really want the place to look any different. It had been his boyhood home and I suppose he didn't want to erase the fond memories he had of it. He was pleased when some old friends told him that the house looked exactly as they remembered it when they were children. This remark sounded innocuous enough, except the people who said it were old enough to have gray hair.

We had to have a heating stove in both the dining and living rooms, to say nothing of Satan, who did his share to warm the kitchen. Nothing less than three stoves would have heated the old house. What we really needed was a basement with a furnace in it, but the house probably wouldn't have stood the stress of such work. So William hauled the heating stoves in every fall and hauled them out every spring.

There were usually two or three weeks in May when the stoves sat there unused, and I would cavil at William to get those ugly things out of the house. He was invariably cautious about removing them, however. His rule of thumb was that the stoves could be taken out only if we hadn't needed a fire for at least three weeks. I would feel like a new woman as soon as I was rid of them and usually launched into a spate of housecleaning. But by the time the weather turned cold in the fall I would welcome these monstrosities back like old friends.

There was one small bedroom that would have made an excellent bathroom—even the landlord agreed on this. But there was no water piped into the house and nothing was ever said about doing this, so the bathroom remained a dream—mine more than the landlord's. It was maddening to think that a few hundred dollars would have saved us from the ignominy of taking baths in the washtub and the need for making all those trips to the Necessary on cold winter nights.

It was even more maddening to think that the landlord had gone to a lot of work and expense to build new horse stalls in the barn when we really didn't need them anymore. The horses were used only for haying and threshing now. They grew heavy coats for winter and the hay shed provided comfort enough for them on all but the coldest nights. But there those sturdy stalls were, built out of lumber so heavy that Dan could have kicked them all he wanted to without making a dent.

Some of the other improvements were needed, however, and they helped a lot. The one barn that had leaned so perilously when we moved there had been straightened and propped up, so that the cattle had a loafing shed on one side and the brood sows a place on the other side. The big hay mound kept all the creatures warm in the winter. And I finally got my new chicken house, complete with plenty of windows and lots of roosting space.

We appreciated everything that was done, of course. What few complaints we had we kept to ourselves. On the days when William was not busy in the fields he helped the landlord with his building and accepted money only once for this. The landlord was almost like a member of the family to us. He was a childless widower so he had never enjoyed that precious gift of a grandchild of his own in his later years. We thought that Don and Bill and Jim sort of helped to fill this gap in his life.

I even thought I understood the landlord's desire to leave the house exactly as it was. Who knows? Maybe he had enjoyed carrying water from the old pump when he was a boy. Maybe he thought everybody liked to take a bath in the washtub. He might not have minded making a midnight trip to the Necessary during a blizzard when he was growing up. To him, those must have been the good old days. If they were good enough for him they ought to be good enough for his tenants. It was just like I'd been saying every since we moved to the farm—it was pigs that counted, not people.

But our landlord wasn't really too anxious to please the pigs, either. They never had a real home anywhere on the place. True, there was a large area in the hay shed where they could go to get out of the bad weather. But this had no separate rooms for the sows when they had their babies. So William had to set up partitions to give them each a place of privacy when their families arrived. The three and four month old pigs didn't fare any better. William put them in the unused horse stalls in the other barn.

So some things had been done, but not everything. The landlord was almost as full of plans as ever, but he told us there were two things on the place that would never change. One of these was the timber, the other the wild hay field. "That timber will never be cleared and that hay field will never be plowed as long as I own this farm," he said on many occasions.

We understood his devotion to the wild hay field, twenty-five acres of virgin prairie grass that had never been touched by a plow. When I walked in this field I knew I was wading across the same grassy sod that Grandfather Lightell had broken with oxen when he first came to the prairie more than a century ago. He had been amazed at the grass then and I was amazed at it now. It could lie all winter under a thick cover of snow and spring to life again with the first warm days. There had never been a drought that would kill it. Each year it reseeded itself. It was impervious to all natural enemies and it did not get eaten off by bugs like the alfalfa sometimes did. It was strong and tenacious and full of life. Only man, with his plow, could tear up its roots and make it die.

However, this hay was too low in protein for the milk cows and we never fed it to them unless we were out of alfalfa. It was coarse and unpalatable to any animal except the horses. I suppose the reason the pioneers thought it was so wonderful was because it was the only hay they had. But we got one cutting of hay off this field every fall and the horses ate it with relish. What was left could be used in place of straw for bedding in the barns.

Timber, Meadow, and Muriel

William knew that the wild hay field would produce many good corn crops if it was plowed up, and he thought the landlord was being overly sentimental in wanting to preserve the prairie grass. But to me it was a link with the past, a living testimony to the land as it had been for hundreds, perhaps thousands, of years. And it was good to know that we could still walk on the same ground that had once known the tramp of moccasined Indians on their way, possibly, to peek in through the windows of the old house.

It was in this field that William saw what appeared to be a wolf, although timber wolves were long thought to be extinct in Iowa. However, conservationists say that it is possible for a large domestic dog to mate with a coyote and produce an offspring bigger than the coyote parent and with the smoky gray color that is characteristic of the wolf. Maybe this is what happened. Whatever the creature was, he was a loner and probably the only one of his kind for miles around.

The landlord's reason for not clearing the timber was that the hills would be too steep to plow even if the trees were cleared off. Actually, the ground there was no steeper than it was in many other places that we were farming. This excuse only served to justify his determination to keep the timber as it was. But we agreed with him on this score. No more hills should be put to the plow. To do so would only have encouraged erosion. Besides, the timber was beautiful and useful. It would have been nothing short of criminal to have cut down its lovely trees.

There was a hundred acres of timber on the place and all the trees native to the Midwest grew there—oak, maple, elm, black walnut, and a few scrubby pines and cedars. The bluegrass in the timber made excellent pasture for the cattle, although they had to walk great distances to get enough to eat. They drank from a spring-fed creek.

The timber abounded with bushes and vines, some of which seemed to have no purpose. Others, like the sumac and the bittersweet, provided a glorious show of color in the fall. The wild gooseberry bushes were the most abundant. Their sour, green berries made excellent pies if you didn't mind getting scratched on their thorns and if you were brave enough to ignore the wasps and bees that were always attracted to them.

He was a loner

Sometimes the wild raspberries bore fruit and sometimes they didn't. Their fruit was smaller than cultivated berries but it was much sweeter. I watched the wild strawberries carefully but never did see a berry on any of the plants, although they grew everywhere.

Picking wild grapes was simple for they grew along the fence lines or around the trunk of trees where they were easy to reach. The grapes made wonderful jelly and sometimes I canned them up for juice. But I discovered that I had to put pectin with them when I made jelly, otherwise I had a gooey concoction that resembled purple molasses.

There were a lot of hazelnut bushes in the timber but we never seemed to have much luck in finding the nuts. They were here today and gone tomorrow. No doubt they were zealously guarded by the squirrels, who were there all the time and knew what was going on. But the nuts, when we could get them, were mild and tasty and not hard to crack.

The black walnuts had to be brought home and spread out so the green hulls would dry before you could get down to the black inner shell that surrounded the nut. These nuts were slightly oily but they had a wonderful flavor when used in cakes or cookies or in fudge and divinity. But it might take an hour to get enough to make anything at all.

We knew that the squirrels hoarded many of the black walnuts, for we saw them every fall toting them away as fast as they could carry them. They knew when the nuts were good and when they weren't, so they simply left the bad ones lying on the ground. We sometimes brought those walnuts home and didn't know they weren't any good until weeks later, when we started in to crack them. It was sad to think that we weren't as smart as the bushy-tailed squirrels but that was the way it was.

The timber was the perfect home for the squirrels. Here they had a plentiful supply of food, lots of trees to skitter about in, and countless branches upon which to build their nests — which were usually about twenty feet off the ground, comfortably wide and deep, and puffy with leaves. Their little ones are born alive and very tiny, but they grow fast on mother's milk and, by the time they leave the nests, are half as big as their parents. The young ones are just as sure-footed on a branch and just as saucy as the older ones, and they can nag just as loudly.

The squirrels owned the timber. Of that there was no doubt in their minds. We were the intruders and they followed us along from tree to tree, scolding us from the time we entered their domain until we left it. William always knew that the last row of corn next to the timber would be husked long before he could get to it. Almost every tree had a few cobs lying under it, mute testimony to the greed of these small creatures.

But the deer also got some of the corn that grew next to the timber. Until a few years previously, we had no deer and nobody was sure what made them come back when they did. But they were there — gentle, shy animals that might be seen among the trees and occasionally around a strawstack that was adjacent to the timber. There were never more than five or six in the herd and they were so beautiful and inoffensive that I never could understand why people wanted to kill them. Yet some men did and took pride in the killing.

No car could reach our timber or any of the fields without first going through the house yard and during the open season I watched carefully to see that no hunters got through. William thought my shoot-if-you-must-this-old-gray-head attitude was very foolish. But I wasn't the least bit ashamed. I thought the timber should be a place of refuge for all the wild creatures, especially the deer. I knew there were many places there for them to hide and the thing to do was to keep the hunters and their guns away.

The timber abounded with bird life, both summer and winter. It was the favorite gathering place for the noisy, black crows, who cawed raucously from the topmost branches of the trees. Some of the cardinals may have migrated south but there were many that stayed with us all winter. In late January, they began singing in defense of their nesting territories. In the summer the meadowlarks seemed to be in constant flight and their liquid songs came unexpectedly from near and far. The tiny goldfinches almost never ventured into the shady vastness of the timber. Perhaps it seemed a fearsome place to them. They were so small. But they lived on the very edge of it in the wild hay meadow, singing their reedy songs from the smaller trees and bushes. Once in awhile, one heard a shrike — his call as sharp and piercing as the long beak with which he impaled hapless field mice and smaller birds on the prongs of the barbed wire fence. But the hawk was the master of all and when he flew over the timber or floated effortlessly on an updraft of air, the voices of all other birds were suddenly stilled.

In May the wild mushrooms sprang up in the timber, seemingly out of nowhere. They were morels, creamy white or spongy brown caps on short stems. A good rain followed by a warm sun would make them jump out of the ground like jack-in-the boxes. They liked the soil around decayed and fallen trees or stumps. But they could grow anywhere — on a barren hillside, in the grass along a fence line, under the gooseberry bushes, amid the compost of last year's dead leaves.

Looking for them was like looking for a needle in a haystack. But there were certain tricks in the hunting. One learned to stand still for several minutes while scanning the ground carefully, visualizing the mushroom in one's mind, imagining it to be there. One trained oneself to look vertically as well as horizontally. There were sometimes twenty or more growing together within a few square feet, yet they were so well camouflaged that it was quite possible to step on one while bending down to pick another.

The mushrooms were often dirty. If it had just rained they were apt to have mud hidden inside their spongy heads, and this had to be cleaned out with the end of a paring knife. Sometimes they were covered with tiny ants. All the mushrooms had to be cut in half and soaked in salt water over night before they could be cooked. If there were ants in them this called for many soakings in brine, plus a long session during which every twist had to be examined. I tried to be careful but I suppose we must have eaten a few ants anyway. Even after the mushrooms had sat all night, there were quite often five or six ants floating in the water.

Any ant I could see got lifted out of the brine, of course, but by this time an ant or two no longer seemed important, for the mushrooms were ready to be drained, rolled in flour, and fried in butter. They were delicious beyond description, very crisp and brown and nutlike in flavor.

We could confidently expect to find morels for two weeks or so each May. Then they would disappear as suddenly as they had come, not to be seen again until the following May. The mushrooms were the small jewels of the timber, and we sought them as assiduously as treasure hunters would have sought gold.

So the timber was a pleasant place to be, and it held many rewards for us, as well as for the cows, the birds, the squirrels, and the deer. We quite agreed with the landlord that this was a place where no changes ought to be made. There was only one thing wrong with the timber. It was hard to get to. You had to start at the long lane north of the house yard, go down a hill through a small pasture, cross the creek, and climb another very large hill before you reached it.

The cows browsed in the timber all day long, and they were usually scattered to kingdom come when it was time to bring them in for milking. William always called them first, hoping they would come of their own volition. They would invariably bellow in answer to him. But this didn't mean they were actually coming. They would have stayed in the timber for a week, even if their udders were bursting with milk. What their bellows really meant was, "Here I am. Come and get me."

To save all that walking — something William detested after he had worked in the field all day — he often drove the tractor out to get the cows.

We had a new tractor now, a sleek, bright red hussy of a thing that was a lot faster than Gertrude could ever hope to be.

We named the new tractor Muriel. Somehow the name seemed to fit, for she was young and beautiful — a far cry from the aged, unlovely, gasoline-stained Gertrude.

Muriel was modern in every respect, and much easier to use. With Gertrude William had had to stop at the ends of the rows when he was cultivating corn. Then he had to use main strength to operate the levers that lifted her ponderous cultivator out of the ground. Otherwise he wouldn't have been able to turn the tractor around. But Muriel performed this chore herself. All William had to do was push a little gizmo and she lifted her cultivator out of the soil and was ready to make another trip across the field. She was much quieter than Gertrude and she didn't belch as much smoke. And it was a lot easier to add or take away her various appurtenances.

Everything she had was bigger and more powerful than what Gertrude had, so William told me. Muriel had lights, too, so he could work in the field as late as he wanted to. And she took to her work with gusto. There was never a murmur of complaint out of her. It was fun to watch when William brought her up over a hill. Her tall exhaust pipe would appear first, like the periscope of a submarine coming out of the water. Then I could see Muriel herself, an eye catcher in her scarlet coat, shining and new, in the first blush of her youth.

However, this did not mean that we had abandoned Gertrude. Far from it. We kept her for odd jobs around the farm, like wood cutting or barn cleaning. When we put up hay she performed the task of drawing the rope through the pulley, so the big forkfuls of leafy hay could be lifted out of the racks and carried into the barn until William yelled "Stop!" Then whoever was driving Gertrude would bring her to a halt, the trip rope would be jerked, and the hay would drop into the loft exactly where it was supposed to be.

Gertrude might not have been as important to us as she once was, yet she still had her place in the scheme of things and we could not have gotten along without her.

Nobody got much of a kick out of riding Gertrude anymore. But Muriel was a novelty and we all wanted to ride her, so we sometimes went along when William went out after the cows in the evenings. He would take Jimmy on his lap and hold one arm around him. Don and Bill and I would stand on the drawbar and hang onto whatever place William told us was safe to hang onto. Then we were off!

I do not know why the boys enjoyed these trips so much, but they did. I suppose part of it was watching their father drive the big red machine, noticing how he put Muriel in gear, how he braked down or speeded up on the hills. (When they got old enough to drive a tractor William discovered that they needed almost no instructions at all.) The best part was trundling across the bridge, which had no railings because they were deemed unnecessary. Any old cow ought to have sense enough not to go too close to the edge, William told me, and they usually did, except every now and then they would engage in shoving matches that brought one or two dangerously close to the brink.

The speed, the hills, and the railless bridge all appealed to our young sons' sense of adventure, I am sure. Me? Well, I just went along for the ride.

But these trips were always pleasurable. They were sort of mini-vacations, little exclamation points of excitement in the ordinariness of our lives.

Chicken Picker-off-ers
and Other Predators

W E had all kinds of predators in the hills—many coyotes, a few foxes, weasels, skunks, raccoons, and even an occasional mink. As long as these creatures kept to the fields and the timber we didn't have to worry about them. But they often came up around the buildings because that was where they could get the most food the easiest.

Their favorite food was chicken. I have no idea how many birds they stole from us throughout the years, but the dollar loss must have been considerable. There wasn't much we could do about it. You just knew that a chicken was going to get "picked off" every now and then, as William phrased it.

Raccoons, weasels, and mink did their thieving at night and very seldom got caught at it. These animals had been known to climb straight up the side of a henhouse in order to slip in at a hole near the roof that was so small nobody thought an animal could possibly get through it. A raccoon, with his long, clawed fingers, could handle a struggling chicken as dexterously as a human could. Weasels and raccoons carried their prey away, but a mink was like Dracula. He drank the blood and left the meat.

The fox was the most daring predator of all. His favorite raiding time was early morning but he wasn't above taking a chicken at any time of day. He would grab a bird and run off so quickly that the terrified chicken scarcely had time to let out a squawk. We would never be entirely sure what had happened unless we found feathers lying out in the field somewhere.

All chickens were supposed to be shut up in the henhouse in the fall and not allowed out until spring. But because they had had freedom to go where they chose all summer, they were loathe to enter prison in the fall. These birds (usually pullets that had yet to lay their first egg) would take to roosting in the trees at night. Thus, they became easy prey for predators. Every fall William and I went through the same ritual with these birds. We would wait until dark, then he would climb a ladder, grab the birds around the legs, and hand them down to me to be carried into the henhouse. William was somewhat less than enamored with this job, however, since he had worked long hours and was tired and sometimes went to bed before the chickens did. Inevitably, a few of these birds got stolen out of the trees before we had rescued them.

Always a light sleeper, I would be wakened by the screeching of a chicken in the night. "There's something after the chickens!" I would say, shaking William awake. "Get the gun and see if you can shoot it." Benumbed by sleep, he would obey before he had time to think, grabbing the gun from the closet and racing outdoors in his pajamas. By the time he got to the trees, the chickens had settled down again and there wasn't a sign of a predator anywhere.

"You must have been dreaming," William would say, as he crept back into bed, shivering. After being roused from a warm bed and chased out into the cold three or four nights in a row, he would let me know that he had had enough of that foolishness. "Don't wake me up in the middle of the night just to save a fifty-cent chicken anymore," he would tell me.

"Then be prepared to get those birds out of the trees tomorrow night," I would retort. "I know I wasn't dreaming. Something was after those birds."

After such a night we always searched the yard for signs of the animal. We found no chicken carcasses and usually no feathers. The total absence of clues only served to reinforce William's contention that I had imagined hearing the squawks in the night. Then one day we stumbled onto the truth.

There was a dead tree standing in the yard not far from the trees where the pullets liked to roost. Its trunk was about twelve feet tall, utterly rotten and useless even for firewood. One day

William hooked a chain around it, fastened the chain to Gertrude's drawbar, and pulled it down so it could be hauled away to a ditch.

When the tree trunk came crashing to the ground we saw that it was hollow inside and this hollow was more than half full of chicken feathers and bones. So the old tree had made a perfect sanctuary for some wily raccoon who had simply dragged his prey down inside where he could dine at leisure. I suppose he had picked off the first bird he had come to. Even then, he would have had to move very fast to carry it down one tree, across ten feet or so of ground, shinny up the rotten tree and drop out of sight.

The raccoon was probably the most intelligent of the predators to inhabit our hills. Occasionally, someone tamed a young one and found him to be an interesting and lovable animal. His expressive, pixie face and amazingly dextrous paws endeared him to his human captors. But raccoons have good memories. Once a friend, always a friend. When he was turned loose to fend for himself he was quite capable of remembering where Those Nice People had lived, and he wasn't above coming back for an occasional midnight snack from their brooder or henhouse.

Knowing that these wild creatures were out there waiting for a chance to steal my chickens was frustrating—the more so because they were often successful. But still they were warm-blooded animals, soft and furry, and fairly intelligent. I could have touched any of them—with the exception of the skunk—gladly enough. After all, they were mammals, just like I was. I had shared a common ancestor with them many millions of years ago and it was only a quirk of evolution that had put them in burrows and me in the house.

This was not true of the snakes, however, whom I considered the most repulsive and most unwelcome of all creatures. The other predators cost us money and the snakes, by killing grain-eating rats and mice, actually saved us money. Yet I would gladly have swapped one snake for six chicken-stealing raccoons, skulking coyotes, or bloodthirsty mink. I had a thing about snakes—a fear that William said was totally unreasonable and unjustified, since they posed no threat to humans. Nevertheless, I worried about them from early May until late October, constantly afraid that I might see one or, worse yet, might not see one until after I had stepped on him.

What we had were big, long bullsnakes, perfectly harmless as snakes go. We saw almost no garter snakes, probably because the bullsnakes ate them. The bullsnakes had a marvelous protective coloring and blended in with whatever they happened to be lying next to. On bare ground they looked brown; on grass they looked green; lying among dead leaves, they were almost indistinguishable from the mottled browns and tans around them. They attained a length of four or five feet at maturity. One could get a good idea of their age while watching them move. The young ones could move with unbelievable speed, while the older ones got fat and lazy and moved much slower. I could have cared less about their longevity, of course. I wished most heartily that they could all die in infancy.

With the first warm days of spring, the bullsnakes got thawed out and they worked their way out of their dens and came to the surface to bask in the sun. Hungry after long months in hibernation, they began to spread out and search for field mice, rats, rabbits, and other snakes smaller than themselves. Their hunger assuaged, they then began to look for mates. It was generally conceded—where there was one snake there were probably two and not too far apart.

I once caught a pair of bullsnakes mating out in the yard. Their tails were pressed together on the undersides and they were writhing in reptilian pleasure, oblivious to my presence. It wasn't until I came very close to them that I saw another snake nearby. He was lying perfectly motionless, his head reared, his cold, unblinking eyes fixed on the mating pair. What amazed me most was the absolute concentration of all three snakes. Ordinarily, they would have seen me coming and would have slithered away very quickly. But during the few minutes in which they were absorbed in this most primal of all urges, they did not even look my way. I ran for the hoe and succeeded in killing two of them.

William and I never agreed on the size of the snakes that I had killed. I invariably thought they were huge. But he always told me they weren't very big at all—simply poor, young, defenseless creatures who should never have left their mothers. The snakes he killed were always big, of course.

Many of our fruit cellars had been built a half century ago and the doors did not fit tightly enough, which practically invited the snakes to come in so they could escape the heat of the summer. Bee once saw a bullsnake hanging from the roof of their cave, his scaly underside clinging to the bricks. I never did understand how a snake could have gotten on the steps of our cave so suddenly one day. He wasn't there when I went into the cellar but he was there when I turned to go. I gathered my skirts high, took the steps at a run, and leaped over him before he knew what was happening.

Bullsnakes are constrictors and simply squeeze to death any small prey like rabbits. One day when I was on my way to the garden I heard a loud, wheezing rale, like an animal struggling for its breath. I had never heard anything like it before and I was hesitant about approaching the weed patch from which the sound came. William was cultivating corn just across the fence and I waved him down, gesturing that there was something frightful going on in the weeds.

He grabbed Gertrude's formidable crank for a weapon and came running, parting the weeds and walking gingerly toward the sound, which was now much weaker. Then he saw them— the tortured rabbit with the bullsnake coiled around it, slowly squeezing it to death. He took a swipe at the snake and it uncoiled and slid away. He held the rabbit up for me to see. Its bones were broken, its body stretched out and covered with saliva. But there was life in the little creature yet, and his feet were twitching spasmodically. William dropped it back in the weeds and hit it on its head to put it out of its misery. Very probably the snake came back later on to finish his meal.

Bob Irving said he had once seen a pheasant wrapped tightly in the coils of a large bullsnake, with the two of them rolling down a hill together. The pheasant hen, who could easily have sailed thirty feet into the air from a sitting position, must have stayed on her nest too long, trying to protect her eggs or her young ones.

But perhaps the snake had first hypnotized the pheasant until she no longer remembered that she had wings with which she could escape. I had always discounted the stories about birds being hypnotized by snakes, until I saw it happen one day.

It was not uncommon to have a snake crawl up into one of the large maple trees in front of the house to rob nests of their eggs or little ones. His presence would alarm the birds and all their happy songs and chirpings would suddenly cease. There would be long periods of silence, punctuated by peculiar warning calls as the birds alerted each other to the danger. I soon learned to interpret these strange calls almost like they had been spoken human words and I knew immediately when the birds were threatened.

One day I heard the there's-a-snake-in-our-tree sound and I went out to locate the trouble. I didn't see the snake but I noticed a lone robin, who seemed glued to his perch. So well camouflaged was the snake that he had to move before I saw him. He was flattened to the limb, inching his way forward. I leaped from the porch and grabbed a stick, but before I had time to throw it, the snake had struck the robin in one swift, blurring movement. I threw the stick, missed the snake but hit the tree limb. The snake was momentarily distracted and relaxed his hold just enough so the robin could get away.

If a bullsnake is cornered and teased he will become angry, rear his head, and emit a vibrant hissing warning from his distended throat. But it takes a while for him to work himself into a snit of bad temper. Usually, he will slither away rather than do battle.

This is not true, however, of the blue racer snake, who is extremely aggressive all the time. We had one field that was low, with a spring-fed creek running through it, and William plowed up a lot of blue racers there every spring. One day he was startled to see a blue racer slither up on the front wheels of the tractor and crawl toward him along the hood. He thought the heat of the hood would surely make the snake jump off, but it didn't. The racer just kept coming toward him and William decided he had better jump off the tractor before he got the snake in his lap.

The blue racers never came near the buildings. William never did see them except in that one field, which was usually too wet to plow until the last of May. Either the racers preferred this dampness or they required longer periods of hibernation than the other snakes. Either way they did not like to be plowed up.

The predators all had their places in the scheme of things. We certainly didn't need the coyotes, the foxes, the raccoons, and the snakes. But they could scarcely be blamed for hunting their own food, even if their methods were reprehensible and the objects of their search were valuable to us. I was ready to do battle with any snake that threatened the beautiful song birds that lived in the house yard. However, I wasn't there to protect them all the time and I knew that the snakes must have robbed many bird nests every spring and no doubt killed a great many adult birds, too.

The robin had been partly to blame for his predicament that day. Robins are lazy birds that like nothing better than to sit. A blue jay would never have sat still long enough to have been hypnotized. He might even have given the snake a few hard pecks from his sharp beak before he flew away. A small quail would have made a good meal for a snake, but it is doubtful if these birds would have stayed around long enough for this to happen. The quail have a strong flocking instinct and when one flies they all fly.

Most of the quail lived in the timber, but there were always a few that stayed around the house. It was fairly easy to call up one of those little brown birds any time of day. All I had to do was whistle the same two flutey notes that he whistled. Invariably I would get an answer. I would wait a few seconds and call again, and he would answer me and come closer. Sometimes I could coax a quail to the ground only a few feet away. He would sit there with his little head cocked to one side, seemingly not frightened of me at all. As long as I sang to him he would sing to me. His look was one of quizzical uncertainty over this featherless, wingless creature with a whistle so like his own. He couldn't seem to figure me out. But I wasn't much good at figuring him out, either. I couldn't tell if I had called in a "he" or a "she." Nor could I tell if the same bird ever came back twice. But their willingness to carry on a flirtation with me had a charming way of making my day.

The only predators that were actively hunted were the coyotes, who were accused of all sorts of dastardly deeds like carrying off little lambs or pigs or killing small calves. When the location of a coyote was known and tracking conditions were good, then the men often went out after him. Brick Nelson would bring his lop-eared hounds, who strained at their leashes and barked like they had the croup. These hounds seemed to confer upon Brick the right to orchestrate the hunt. He would tell everybody where to go and what gulch to guard. Then they were off—the men, the hounds, and the hapless coyote. There would be much loud shouting from hill to hill and so many rifle shots coming from so many different directions that I never could figure out how the men avoided being caught in their own cross fire. And the coyote, who zigged when the hunters zagged and could get himself out of the most ungodly predicaments, usually got away unscathed.

I was happy when the coyote got away. I was disgusted with these hunts. I thought them cruel and unnecessary. It didn't do much good to kill one coyote because there were always others to take his place. Besides there was always the chance that it was a mother with hungry pups that would starve if she didn't come back to her den. But it was the thought of one, small, thirsty animal being chased relentlessly for miles and miles while beleaguered by enemies on every side that bothered me the most.

My sympathies were always with the coyote. I therefore developed a lasting grudge against Brick's ugly, salivating hounds, who panted so hard their tongues hung practically to their knees. I always thought it would have been nice if there had been enough coyotes to have turned the tables and chased the hounds for a change.

Helping Out

ALL farm women in my day were expected to do what was euphemistically known as "help out." Translated, this meant that you were supposed to do all the work that your husband didn't have time for, didn't like to do, or considered beneath the dignity of a man.

A good farm wife was worth her weight in gold, even though she might not have a dime in her pocket that she could call her own at the end of the year. A poor farm wife — one that couldn't or wouldn't carry her share of the work burden — was like a millstone around her husband's neck.

I realized early on that I might qualify for the latter, dubious honor. Sure, I raised chickens, I washed, I ironed, I cooked, I baked bread and had, meanwhile, produced a goodly number of sons. Still, I knew I wasn't helping out like I should and I decided it was time I put my shoulder to the wheel, which had been turning with agonizing slowness and sometimes seemed not to be turning at all. After much thought, I came up with the answer. I would raise a big, really big garden.

The seed catalogues made it all sound so easy. Juicy melons, tempting asparagus, succulent green peas, golden carrots, and zesty radishes could all be produced from a few pennies worth of seed. That's what the books said. They never said anything about aphids, mealy bugs, beetles, grasshoppers, striped worms, smooth green worms, or big brown worms with fuzz.

The seed catalogues always had big pictures of satisfied women beaming proudly at the tremendous results they had achieved with a mere handful of seeds. On the left hand page, one might find a woman standing haughtily beside a pile of pumpkins that averaged thirty-seven pounds each. On the right hand page, one might find another woman, fondly holding an armful of carrots, any one of which was big enough to feed a family of five. You only had to turn a page to find another woman gloating over a watermelon so big that her husband had had to ask help from a neighbor to lift it into the wagon.

All of these women had written enthusiastic letters to the seed companies, saying things like, "I couldn't garden without your seeds!" "Your seeds are the greatest!" "I'll never buy seeds from anyone else!" Not one of these women said anything about sunburn, calluses, skinned knees, or aching backs. But then they were all old pros, who knew the Farmer's Almanac from cover to cover and could spot a weevil at thirty paces.

The catalogues kept using the same pictures year after year. It got to be a little boring. But after I had gardened for a while, I was very happy to look at these same old pictures every spring. It was nice to know that hoeing hadn't killed me between one catalogue and the next.

I started out gardening with high hopes, but no matter how assiduously I pushed the clods around I never succeeded as a gardener. However, I did set a few records.

Nobody ever raised a hotter radish. I did all the right things to them—got the seed in early, thinned out the rows, hoed them faithfully. They got the same rain and the same sunshine that everybody else's radishes got. But my neighbors' turned out to be crisp and mild while mine burned with an unquenchable fire all the way down. William, a confirmed radish lover, refused to eat them.

My tomatoes hung like green warts behind listless leaves all summer long, as if they were ashamed to come out and show themselves in the light of day. They set all records for slow growth. Every summer it was the same thing. Which would come first? The ripe tomato? Or the frost? Nine times out of ten it was the frost.

When I planted onion seeds the little plants came up as thick as the hair on a dog's back and not much bigger. I thinned the plants relentlessly, just like everyone told me to do, so the plants would have room to grow. They made some elegant tops but the onions themselves seldom got any bigger than a lead pencil. I tried putting out onion sets but never achieved an adult onion that was much bigger than the set was when I put it out.

I could raise peas, however, so I went in heavily for them. But it took a couple of hours to pick them off the vines, shell them, and cook them. An enormous bowlful would disappear in a matter of minutes.

William wisely planted the potatoes and the sweet corn out in the field somewhere so he could tend them with the tractor cultivator. With these things we had better luck. We rivaled any pen of pigs you ever saw, the way we ate corn off the cob. We feasted on this delicious stuff as long as it lasted. But I didn't like to can it and William refused to eat it cut off the cob anyway, so we merely enjoyed it while we could and then waited for next year's crop to come around.

All this gardening took lots of time and effort, and I didn't seem to be getting anywhere with it. William, who preferred baking powder biscuits to anything that grew in the garden, could have cared less when I failed. But I was ashamed of myself and I developed little ways to shield myself from the neighbors' scorn. I trained myself not to snatch when people offered me something out of their gardens. "How nice of you to give me such lovely tomatoes," I would say. "Mine aren't ripe yet." Or, "Thanks so much for the squash and onions — mine aren't quite big enough yet." I knew full well that nothing I raised was ever going to be big enough or ripe enough, ever.

Once I raised some nice broccoli with nary a sign of a bug on it. When I went out to cut some I found the heads almost eaten up by long green worms that blended in with the broccoli so well I had to get right down and stare at it before I could see them. I could tolerate bugs but those worms really got to me. I tried cabbage just once. Too many worms. Bugs weren't so bad. There was much to commend in a good, hard-shelled bug that didn't make you scream if he happened to get on you.

It made me tired just to look at the hoe. I compared myself to the other women and knew that I couldn't light a candle to them. They thrived on work. They were busy all day long. Not just busy, but *Busy Busy*. There wasn't a laggard among them and there wasn't a husband among them who hadn't gotten the price of his marriage license back a hundred thousand fold from his water-toting, egg-gathering, pea-picking spouse.

Bee Bagley was a prime example. Her real name was Bea. But the way she buzzed and flitted around doing her work closely resembled that estimable insect, and she was forever "Bee" in my mind. By eight o'clock in the morning she would have already tended the chickens, cooked a breakfast consisting of oatmeal, pancakes, sausage and eggs, done the dishes, washed the forty-three parts of the cream separator, made the bed, swept the floor, dusted the furniture, and maybe hoed a couple of rows in the garden.

If you dropped in on her at eight o'clock in the morning you would have expected to find her in a dirty dress with her sneakers untied and her hair askew. However, you would find her clean, combed, and full of pep, probably in the process of whipping up a little something for dessert—like an angelfood cake, now that her hens were laying so well that she could use fourteen egg whites in an angelfood because she could make a jelly roll out of the yolks later so nothing would be wasted.

It would have been nice if Bee had panted a little, out of common decency if nothing else. But no, here she was with all that energy, in spite of the fact that she had been in poor health for several years and was dead certain that her "ute-russ" was in the wrong place. She knew she ought to go to Mayo's and find out about that pesky uterus, she often said, except that she didn't want to leave all the work for Chris to do alone. I couldn't understand where she got all her energy. Not when it made me tired just to look at the hoe.

One day Bee stopped for a visit—not for long, mind you—because she had lots of work to do at home. She was having hay men for dinner the next day, she told me, sitting on the sofa and smoothing down her homemade dress. She had a nervous tic, an almost imperceptible jerking of the head which plagued her at intervals and agitated the feather on her hat. Yet she was a handsome woman, tanned from working outdoors, and her brown eyes sparkled when she talked.

As soon as the hay men left she intended to get right busy on her pickled carrots, she told me. It seemed she always had so many carrots she didn't know what to do with all of them, and after she'd canned thirty quarts and put a couple of bushels down in sand for the winter she always made up a dozen jars of pickled carrots.

My carrots weren't doing a thing. Not a thing, I complained.

I had made the remark innocently enough but it was just like I had waved a red flag in front of a bull. Bee jumped up at once and said she'd take a look at my garden and tell my why my carrots weren't doing anything.

Now my garden was nothing you ever wanted to show to anybody. It was an aberration, an abomination. It was something you instinctively wanted to hide, like gangrene or your notes at the bank. But I could see that Bee was bound and determined to see my garden. I had opened up my big mouth and the cat was out of the bag. Mentally, I flagellated myself every step of the way out there.

For a few minutes she just stood, looking around and saying nothing. I could see she was nonplussed. Nay, she was stunned.

"How much manure do you put on your garden?" she asked finally.

"None," I confessed.

"That's your first mistake and probably your biggest mistake," she said. "You can't raise a garden without manure. Your ground hasn't been worked well enough. Your clods are too big. You ought to hoe every day and never let the weeds get ahead of you like that. Every single weed saps the strength from your plants."

Finally, she got to the carrots. She let go with a barrage of advice from which I plucked several gems: you didn't thin your carrots well enough—they're too thick in the row; your carrots are too near your tomatoes—carrots won't do a thing if they're near large plants; you must have planted them too early or too late—the right time being during the full moon about thirty-six days after your sycamore begins to bud.

I made a mental note not to mention carrots again to anybody. Not only carrots, but cucumbers, radishes, beets, onions, spinach, and God Knows How Many Other Vegetables.

I made one last effort to redeem myself. "My green beans are doing awfully well, aren't they?" I asked, motioning toward the vines that were practically dripping with long, crisp pods.

Bee disposed of my green beans with one short sentence. "Any old fool can raise green beans," she said.

With that parting shot Bee decided it was time she was getting along. Heaven only knew she had plenty of work to do, she said, and she wasn't one to put off until tomorrow what she could do today. She got into her car, gave me her most understanding smile, and said brightly, "Come over and see me sometime. I'll show you *my* carrots."

And with that she was off, driving right through a bevy of molting hens that had been dusting themselves in the yard. They squawked in alarm and took to flight, loosing a small blizzard of white feathers that floated in the air long after the birds had settled down again.

I waited a couple of weeks before I went to see Bee's garden and might not have gone then except she called to tell me that she had some ripe tomatoes I could have. I'll do anything, I thought to myself. I'll praise. I'll grovel—anything to get a juicy, honest-to-God, sun-ripened tomato. So I went.

Obviously, she meant to show me her whole garden—a thing of perfection—fecund, weedless, heavy with the fruits of her summer's labor. I must see it all, down to the very last bean. She led me up one row and down the other, her face beaming with pride.

I damned near ran out of adjectives.

Once, when I had foolishly row-hopped in an effort to save time, she took me firmly by the arm and pulled me back, like a plough horse being jerked backed in its proper row of corn, and she said, "You don't want to miss my winter radishes! They're just coming up now."

At last we got to her carrots, their fernlike tops still green and growing. Bee tugged hard on the foliage of one plant but the carrot refused to budge, even after she wiggled it back and forth several times. Finally, she dug around the root with her fingers, scraping the supporting soil away. Then and only then did she succeed in dislodging the carrot. Proudly, she held it up for me to see. It was a great, hunkering, obscene phallus of a thing with long brown root hairs blowing in the breeze. It would have taken ten of my spindly carrots to have made one of Bee's.

Eventually, I gave up on the smaller stuff like carrots, lettuce, and onions, and went on to bigger things. I decided that I would try raising some berries. It cost more to get started with them but once a bed was established it was supposed to last for years. But first you had to get a bed started; easier said than done, I discovered.

One spring I ordered two dozen red raspberry plants. They arrived in good shape and we set them out with high hopes. Next year we would have all the juicy red berries we wanted — that was what we thought. But the plants never produced a berry that next summer or any of the following summers. I pruned them, I hoed them, and kept the weeds down. No amount of fussing would bring berries. All we ever had were bushes with thorns.

Intrigued by the pictures of big, red strawberries in the seed catalogues, I ordered a hundred plants. They all grew and made foliage like crazy. But they never produced any fruit, even the third year after they were set out.

In desperation, I turned to Bee, who was always up to her ankles in ripe strawberries every June, and asked her to come over and see what the trouble was. She strode through the patch, stopping here and there to inspect a few plants and occasionally harumphing in disbelief. For once, the omniscient Bee was stumped to the point of speechlessness.

"Well, what's the trouble?" I asked irritably, expecting this neighborhood oracle to come up with an immediate judgment.

"I don't really know," she said. "Your plants all look healthy but they aren't making runners like they should be doing at this time of the year."

"Maybe I set them out in the wrong time of the moon," I remarked acidly.

"No, I think your problem goes deeper than that," Bee answered. "I think the nursery goofed up somewhere. It looks to me like you might have all male or all female plants, which means that there isn't any fertilization taking place. That explains why you don't have any berries. The smart thing to do is plow this patch up and start all over again with new plants."

The Chinese have the Year of the Horse and the Year of the Dog. But once I had the Year of the Watermelon.

Now, a muskmelon is something you can plant and confidently expect to eat before you get so old you have to enter the rest home. Every muskmelon will produce a lot of runners and all these runners will have adorable little melons on them in a matter of weeks. By fall you will have so many ripe muskmelons that you won't know what to do with them and you may find yourself giving them away to people you don't even like just so you can get rid of them.

But watermelons are something else again. They get very big, so they need a lot of time to grow to maturity. During the last two weeks it is always nip and tuck with the frost. We were undaunted with these minor details, however, and one year we planted seventy-five hills of watermelons. Practically every seed grew and the vines quickly covered the ground. William, who was never much impressed with my gardening—and not without reason—thought the melon patch looked great.

"All you have to do now is hoe them and keep the weeds down," he said. "And be sure to keep the bugs off. I hope it won't frost too early this fall, otherwise the melons won't get ripe."

I spent half of my time that summer hoeing the melon patch. The other half I spent bending over the plants, derriere uppermost, my face streaming sweat, while I used one hand to separate the leaves and the other hand to sprinkle on the stinking bug dust. The bugs took a lot of killing. Although the label on the can proclaimed how deadly the stuff was, I noticed a lot of bugs waddling knee deep in poison with no deleterious effects on their health or mobility.

It was a long, hot summer. But, come fall, the big, smooth green melons lay everywhere, their glossy backsides soaking up the late summer sun. William considered himself the only qualified melon thumper in the family and he made daily visits to the patch, rapping on the melons with his knuckles and listening for that deep hollow sound that would indicate ripeness. It wouldn't be long now, he reported, after one of these inspections. If the frost would just hold off. . . .

But of course it didn't. Days had been warm and sunny but as soon as the sun went down it cooled off quickly. One night the frost came and disposed of our melons in one fell swoop, killing the vines and making any further development impossible. Stripped of their covering leaves, the melons lay like green tombstones all over the garden. All those weeks of hoeing and bug dusting had been for naught. We loaded up the melons and threw them into the hog pens, where they were eaten with relish down to the last rind.

It was all very discouraging. It was too late to demand a refund from the nurseries for the berry plants. Besides, nobody could refund the time and effort wasted on these projects. I had spent three or four summers on the berries, and one on the watermelons and had accomplished nothing. One expected to lose some time, like when the jelly didn't jell and had to be boiled over again. But to lose whole summers? It was maddening.

So I wasn't really "helping out" yet. I couldn't milk a cow, like Henrietta or Lolly or that wisp of a Eunice could. I couldn't pick, shell, and can twenty pints of peas in a day like Mary McCrilley could. If I managed to decapitate, defeather, and dress out six roosters in a day, I was pooped. By no stretch of the imagination could I have dressed out twenty-five roosters and got them ready for the freezer in one day, like Bee could.

William kept telling me that this was because I hadn't gotten toughened in to work yet. But I gathered that this process took a long time and had to begin early, maybe the first day you came home from kindergarten. I was pushing forty now and I hadn't gotten the hang of gardening yet and it appeared that I never would. I came out of all of this with the firm conviction that gardeners are born — not made.

But then some of this didn't really seem to be my fault. Why, for instance, was I the only woman in the neighborhood to have unisex strawberries? I was never able to figure that out. I seemed to be a female personification of Murphy's law: if anything can go wrong it will.

William told me not to worry about not being able to raise a big garden. "When Jimmy is old enough to go to school you can help me with the farm work," he said. This was a very comforting thought. Now I had something to look forward to.

Where the Grass Is Greener

TRUE to his word, William put me to work outdoors as soon as all three boys were in school. No, it is not quite fair to say he "put me to work." He would never have forced me to do a man's work. What I did was done because I wanted to do it. I had often told him that I wished I were a man, so that I could have something interesting and challenging to do for a change. Housework was boring, I would tell him.

"What makes you think that a man's work isn't boring?" he would ask me.

"Because. You don't do the same things year in and year out," I would answer.

"Remember, I have to plow for a month every spring. Wouldn't you say that might be boring?"

"No, because when you're done with the plowing you go on to something else."

"What about milking the same cows twice each day for three hundred and sixty-five days of the year? Don't you suppose I get tired of that?" he would ask.

I had to agree that William had a point there and I should have conceded the logic of his argument and given in gracefully. But I didn't. I continued to look over the fence and I was certain that the grass was greener on the other side. For several years I seem to have been poised between a man's world and a woman's world, longing to be in the one while forced to be in the other. William had wisely recognized the depth of my discontent over the years and he was simply offering me a way out.

No doubt he believed that (a) I could take the place of one

of the neighbor men when he needed help, or (b) that I would soon have my fill of hard work and would come back to the kitchen fully convinced that a woman's place was in the home. Of course, there was the possibility that his motivation was neither "a" or "b" but was, instead, "c." This stood for the work he didn't want to do himself.

My very first job turned out to be a "c" job. William assigned me the task of setting up oat shocks in a low corner of one field where the sunflowers had grown up right along with the oats. The sunflowers had tremendous stalks at least six feet tall. They were stiff and hard and they kept knocking my hat off. Within the hour I was tired and my back was aching. I noticed that William had set up ten shocks to my one and he was far away from me in the field. But I got all the shocks set up. He really appreciated my help, William told me when we came in for lunch. I politely said I was glad to be of help and mentioned nothing about being given a "c" job on my first day out.

So I started out at the age of forty, or thereabouts, on a new, part-time career. In the field, I amounted to about one-half of a man, William told me. This was because I was neither big nor strong and I had an almost imbecilic approach to machinery. Gertrude was too hard to handle and I never drove her at all. Muriel was too fast and powerful for me. I never felt I had her under control — and William knew I didn't. I made him nervous when I drove her through a gate because he knew I was quite capable of taking a post and several yards of fence with me. If I could have driven Muriel then William could have driven Gertrude and we could have gotten our cultivating done in half the time. But given Muriel and a full tank of gas, I probably would have uprooted four rows of corn all the way from Woodbine to Des Moines.

So we both recognized my limitations early on. There were really only two jobs that I ever became proficient at: oats cutting and shocking, and wood sawing. During those times my husband was glad to have the help of this half-a-man woman.

Although combines were rapidly being put into use, our neighborhood continued to thresh oats — in part because you had a huge pile of bedding straw left after the threshing was done. But this meant that our oats had to be cut with a binder,

My first "C" job

set into shocks, and allowed to dry out thoroughly before they were threshed. I was pressed into service as a binder operator. This I could do because all I had to do was operate a few levers.

The binder, pulled by the tractor, consisted of a large reel that rotated and brushed the oats into a sickle that cut them off and let them fall onto the moving platform. Then they were carried along to a part of the machine that bound them into neat, compact bundles and eventually spewed them out on the ground. I sat atop the binder with my left foot firmly strapped into a pedal that was attached to a rod on the bundle carrier. It was my job to watch the carrier and, when four or five bundles lay on it, I pulled my foot up, thus tripping the carrier so the bundles would fall off. We would come along later and set these bundles into "shocks," as they were called.

It was also part of my job to listen for any suspicious sounding noises that would indicate trouble in the binder's unpredictable innards. I was supposed to watch for any deviations in the working of the sickle, the reel, the canvas platform, and all the gears I could see. If I heard anything unusual I was supposed to yell at William immediately, so he could stop before a serious breakage occurred.

Any breakage was serious, took time to repair, and cost money. Our binder was old and possessed dozens of moving parts, all of which were indispensable and prone to break. It clattered, clanked, and rattled. But then this was the nature of the beast, and I soon learned to differentiate between the normal clatters, clanks, and rattles, and the abnormal ones. Every hour or so William would stop and squirt grease on every piece of metal that moved. This helped, but it was no great panacea, and we were lucky indeed to get through a whole day of oats cutting without having a breakdown.

Most old binders and threshing machines have been scrapped now. Very soon they will become something that can be seen only in a museum. But sometimes even now, the whole process is done just so people can see how threshing was in the "old days." Invariably, this process will be shown on one of the local television stations. Everything and everybody will be there—the threshing machine, the hayracks, the horses, the men who pitch the bundles into the machine, and the spectators, who marvel at the way things used to be. It is all very fine and educational and interesting. However, these spectators and TV viewers will have missed half the fun. The women will never know the hustle and bustle that went into preparing food for fifteen or sixteen hungry men. The children will never know the excitement of seeing the threshing machine come chugging down the road on its way to their place. The men will never know the satisfaction of hauling in a big load of bundles and pitching them into the thresher. There was a lot of work that went along with threshing time. Yet there was a lot of good-natured camaraderie among the men of the crew and the farmer's wife and neighbor woman who came to help her do the cooking. And there was always a great sense of accomplishment when the job was done and the bins were full of golden oats.

I always enjoyed riding the binder. There was a big umbrella that bolted on the back of the seat and cool breezes blew under it all day. But things were different when Don and Bill got old enough to ride the binder. Then I shocked the grain and was out in ninety-degree heat all day long.

To be a good shocker you had to be able to set up shocks that wouldn't blow down. Speed was important because newly cut oats went through a "sweat" and got damp, and they cured better if you got the heads off the ground. Besides, you didn't want the oats to get drenched with rain. A shock consisted of seven to ten bundles of oats, their stiff bottoms firmly set on the ground, their fluffy heads together at the top. The tight round shocks looked like little tepees scattered around the field.

As a shocker, William had to admit that I was as good as he was. My shocks stood up bravely to the strongest wind and they were uniform and compact. And I was fast. One year when we had a hundred acres of oats I walked behind the binder and set up the shocks as soon as they came off the carrier so when William stopped the tractor for the last time we were all shocked up. My back ached and my hands were blistered. I was dirty and soaked with sweat, just as I was within ten minutes of my arrival in the field every day. But it was a good feeling to know that we were done and when I looked around the field and saw all the tidy little tepees, I knew it had all been worth it.

I never got the lure of making those tepees out of my blood. Whenever we drove through oats country where the un-cut grain was especially heavy, William would look at me and say, "How would you like to set up some shocks in *that* field?"

"I'd just love it," I would answer. "Simply love it."

There was one other time of year when I did a man's work and enjoyed every minute of it. This was in the fall when we went to the timber to cut our winter's supply of wood.

We had a buzz saw, a heavy, unwieldy contraption with a thirty-inch, round blade and a wide carriage to hold the logs, all of which bolted across Gertrude's ample chest. Power flowed to the saw by means of a belt that ran off a pulley near one rear wheel. When all the bolts were fastened so the blade was tight, then William put it in gear and the blade turned with blinding speed.

He stood on one side of the saw, I on the other. He lifted a log onto the carriage and shoved it over until a length suitable for Satan or the heating stoves could be brought against the blade. Ever so carefully, and with equal pressure on both ends of the log, we brought it back and let the saw go through it. A chunk of wood could be cut off in a few seconds. It was my job to hang onto this chunk as it was being cut and then toss it to the wagon on my left. This was called "off-bearing."

It was dangerous work and you had to know what you were doing. You had to make sure that your hands were kept away from the saw and that you didn't stumble and fall into that murderous blade. It could sever a hand or arm instantly. (A woman who lived a few miles away had lost an arm this way.) Because of greater proximity to the saw, the off-bearer was in greater danger than the one who handled the long end of the log. And there was danger even if you didn't trip and fall into the saw. Occasionally, the blade would break and pieces would go hurtling off to God only knew where. Where they hit they hit, and there was no chance to dodge one of these dangerous missiles.

The work was hard but exhilarating, and I enjoyed it. I liked the precision with which I could grab a chunk of wood, toss it into the wagon without looking (there was no time to look) and grab the next chunk of wood, and give it a toss—with no change in rhythm.

One time I got carried away, applied too much muscle, and threw a huge amount of wood completely over the wagon, where it landed on the ground on the other side. William, who was facing that direction, saw what I was doing, but he didn't tell me. He thought it was a big joke; so did I. We had many a chuckle over this long after my wood sawing days were over.

And I wish they weren't over. Gertrude, and William and I had a good thing going in those days. Nothing would make me any happier than to step up to that saw again.

There was one fringe benefit from my wood cutting. If two men went out to saw wood they were often inclined to get in a hurry and the wood that came back was sometimes in such large chunks that it was hard to get them in Satan's relatively small firepot. And this was perfectly understandable. Wood sawing took a lot of time and one hated to ask too much of one's neighbor, who might not saw any wood for himself at all and so would not be able to collect in kind for the labor he had contributed. So the inclination was to shove that log through in order to get the job done, with the result that a lot of chunks came out longer than they should have been. But this didn't happen when I was there. My work was free and we did not have to hurry. If I saw a chunk that was too long I would yell at William over the whine of the buzz saw and tell him so. We simply ran it through again and cut it in half.

Working outdoors gave me a better understanding of why William preferred quiet evenings at home. After a long day in the field or the timber it was a great relief just to sit and do nothing. I knew now that the grass wasn't nearly as green on the other side of the fence as I had thought it was. But the small jobs that I helped with were a lot more challenging than shaking the dust mop, and for once I felt like I was making some worthwhile contributions.

We always cut wood during the sunny days of late September and early October, days when the air was as clear as blown glass and cottony clouds floated on a sapphire sea. The timbered land lay black and moist under crisp, gold and russet leaves that rustled like taffeta when we walked through them. A few bees—caught between honeymaking and hibernation, and strangely disinclined to sting—would circle aimlessly around us. Each day seemed like a special act of creation, a lustrous pearl produced by nature in a rare mood of benevolence.

But we knew that the days of Indian summer were numbered. Soon the rains would fall and the snow would not be far behind. Then one day nature would turn on us like a vixen, lashing us with cold winds, whipping snow into crystalline mountains, and driving us to cover—as if she wanted all humans out of her sight.

But long before this happened William would have everything ready for winter—tar paper on the north side of the henhouse, extra bedding straw hauled in from the field, dirt piled along the water pipes to keep them from freezing. Later on, a barrel would be sunk into the stock tank and a fire built in it to keep the water reasonably warm. If this sounds like a primitive arrangement it's because it was. But it was the only system we had and the other farmers did the same thing. I don't think electric heaters for stock tanks had been invented yet, and if they had been, we probably wouldn't have used them. A barrel with some cobs and wood burning in it served the purpose very adequately and the cattle and horses didn't know the difference. So these precautions took care of the barn creatures.

When they were all clustered together, animal heat would take care of the rest, William assured me.

We still had ourselves to think about, however. But about all we could do was make sure we had plenty of fuel and groceries on hand and try to avoid sickness or accident, either one of which would pose serious problems during a blizzard.

One of the drawbacks in living in the old house at the end of the lane was the fact that we were off the main road by almost a mile. Our lane almost always drifted full, although there was never a good explanation as to why it did. Snow fencing did not seem to help. The drifts were just as high with it as without it. William did a lot of manual scooping but sometimes the drifts were too much for him, in which case Gertrude and her scoop were put to work. If the snowbanks proved too much for the doughty Gertrude, then we had to wait until the county snowplow came, which might take several days, because the main roads were always cleared first.

So the old house at the end of the lane was thoroughly isolated during a bad blizzard and we didn't have a much better chance of escaping from it than we would have had trying to flee Alcatraz. But being snowbound was not all bad, if everyone stayed well. The danger lay in being out during a bad blizzard, which is what happened once to William, Don, and Bill. We all had several anxious hours during which we wondered if they would ever get home again.

Snowbound

THAT January day began harmlessly enough. The sun was shrouded by heavy gray clouds and the air was damp, but there were no signs that a blizzard was brewing when the boys went off to school that morning. It started to snow about ten o'clock, big flakes more indicative of an ordinary snowfall than a blizzard. By eleven the snowfall was much heavier; the wind was roaring in from the north and driving the snow straight ahead, so by looking at it one wondered if it would light anywhere or just keep blowing on forever.

Indeed, this hard, steady wind that blew for more than forty hours without any detectable change in velocity or direction was a characteristic of this blizzard. This was what piled the drifts so high and made the storm one of the worst in many years.

Winter choring takes time under the best of conditions, but at a time like this there is a greater sense of urgency about these routine tasks. William was out almost all morning and when he came in, he said that he should have known a storm was brewing by the nervous way the cattle had acted the day before. They sensed bad weather long before it reached us, he remarked.

I had never believed this theory and told him I thought it belonged with old wives' tales, and there couldn't be any more credence in it than the myth about the thickness of the fuzz on a caterpillar being related to the severity of the coming winter. But he always insisted that cattle were prescient when it came to storms. This was especially noticeable just before a thunderstorm, when they would run or mill about and a mild-mannered cow might suddenly take to butting the others. He had seen this happen so many times that he no longer had any doubt about it, he told me.

But there was no argument about how the barn creatures were reacting to this storm. The horses took refuge under the lean-to of the hayshed and the cows were loath to leave the barn when William herded them out to drink. They turned their backs to the wind, hunkered down around the tank, then hurried back inside, the wind too sharp even for their thick hides.

By one o'clock the snow was drifting badly and William decided that he would have to bring the boys home from school. The situation was worsening so fast, he said, that he would be lucky if he didn't get stuck somewhere on the way.

"Maybe you should walk through the field and bring them back on foot," I suggested. "It isn't so far that way."

"Woman," he said in exasperation, "you don't have any idea what it's like out there. Those boys can't walk in a wind like this. Besides, we'd have to cross the creek and we couldn't tell where to cross. Anyway, it's dangerous to be out in the open field in a blizzard. We'll be a lot safer in the car on the road. Now get me a blanket to take along, in case we get hung up in a drift somewhere."

When William called me "Woman" I knew that further remonstrations on that particular subject were out of the question. He wanted no advice and would tolerate no suggestions from me. I was given no more credence than one of the squaws Evalina had seen plodding along behind her pony-riding spouse so many years ago. Strangely enough, I did not mind. William asserted himself so forcefully and called me "Woman" only when he knew that a situation was dangerous and his judgment was best. I resented the word not one whit. Sometimes it was very comforting to know who the chief was. So, meek as the proverbial lamb, I went for the blanket.

He got in the car and left at once, the snow flying in all directions as he hit the drifts with all the power our old Chevy had. So far, so good, I thought to myself when he got through the first one. He just might make it through. But there were three miles to go yet and the school road had a propensity for drifting, for much of it was narrow and low and invited the snow.

Snow or no snow, fuel and water had to be brought into the house and I made several trips outdoors to get it. It was almost impossible to walk against the wind and it blew through my many layers of clothing as though they weren't there. But I did not stop until Satan's reservoir was filled and there was extra water for whatever else we might need. I topped off each arm load of wood with two or three extra chunks, until I almost staggered under the weight. When the woodbox was full and there was a big stack piled on the porch I decided I surely had enough fuel in to last until the morrow, when William would be home to carry some more.

Or would he? At three o'clock I was beginning to wonder, for there were still no signs of my family. Small Jimmy and I stood at the kitchen window and watched anxiously up the road. Whipped by the wild wind, the snow was amassing in higher and higher drifts. In the swirling whiteness it was hard to tell how deep it was — until you noticed that most of the fence posts had disappeared and there was only a brown tip here and there to mark the fenceline. No car could possibly get through snow that deep, and I knew for a certainty that wherever William and the boys were they must surely be in trouble.

I tried to call Bee, for they would have to pass the Bagley house on their way. I could scarcely turn the crank on the old wall phone and there were ominous crackings and hummings on the line. I shouted into the phone, hoping that somebody — anybody — would hear me. But there was no answer. I slammed the receiver back, angry at this little brown box that would so faithfully carry all the inconsequential chatterings of an ordinary day, yet fail me now.

The radio was no help, either. All I heard was that temperatures were low and winds were high — as if anybody had to be told about that.

At four I bundled up again, pulled on my boots and mittens and started for the henhouse to gather the eggs. When I got to the point where I could see the building I knew I was whipped. A huge drift embraced the henhouse like a cold, white arm. Only a few feet of windows on the south side were visible and the door was completely blocked off. The eggs would have to freeze. Obsessed with the idea that I must have all the fuel on hand that I possibly could, I loaded my arms with wood and fought my way back to the house. After that abortive trip I realized more than ever how desperate the situation was and what a struggle William must be having to bring the children home. Surely by this time they would have had to abandon the car. They would be on foot, nearly blinded by snow yet having to stay on the road no matter what, because to get off the road could be fatal. It was not quite dark yet but I turned the yard light on anyway, comforted because I had done something that might help.

My family was not home at five o'clock, nor at six, and I was frantic with worry. There was no let up in the wind and the snow was so heavy that the yard light was scarcely visible thirty feet away. The night was pitch dark now and I could not see how anyone could possibly find his way in it. I caught myself praying the same prayer over and over again. "Please, God, bring my family home. Please bring my family home."

Keeping the three stoves fueled and preparing supper helped to keep me busy and I set the table with a noisy clatter of plates and silverware, as if these homey sounds could dispel the gloomy ghosts that raced around in my mind.

Young though he was, four-year-old Jimmy understood the seriousness of the situation and he had stood guard at the kitchen window for hours. So it happened that he was the one who saw them first. "Hey, Mom," he said. "There's something moving out there."

And indeed there was something moving out there. A wide, dark, shadowy form that resembled a huge bat with its wings outstretched was just coming into the faint glow of the yard light. William, his tall frame bent to the wind, was in the middle, and he had a boy on either side. All three were enveloped as one with the blanket.

Oblivious to the cold, I ran to the porch to greet them. "Thank God you're home," I cried. "I was afraid you would get lost and freeze to death."

"There were times when I thought we would never make it home alive," William answered.

I cried with pity when I saw my family. Their faces were

raw and red from cold. Their coats and mittens were thick with snow and their feet so nearly frozen that they did not want to take another step on them after they came into the house. Don and Bill were too tired to talk. Even William was exhausted. The boys had been brave through it all, William told me. They didn't cry until we began to take off their boots and shoes. Then the tears came.

He had gotten thoroughly stuck on his way to school, William said, and shoveling out had consumed a great deal of time before he even got to the schoolhouse. He had gotten stuck twice more on the way back, the last time when it was already getting dark. That was when he had decided to abandon the car and walk the last two miles. The wind had been so strong that they had trouble breathing, so the blanket had been a godsend. Only by holding a corner of it over their noses could they manage to get their breath. When it was possible, William had gone ahead and made a path for the boys, but when they came to the really big drifts he had simply carried them through. He thought he must have carried them almost half the way.

"Thank God you are big and strong," I said.

"I was never so grateful for my strength in my whole life as I was today," he said. "This storm is the worst I've ever seen for years, and I hope I never have to be out in anything like it again. I considered stopping at Bagleys overnight but the boys wanted to come home."

"The boys wanted to come home." That simple statement brought tears to my eyes again. Humble though the old house at the end of the lane was, it must have represented something very precious to our eight-year old and our ten-year old to make them willing to undergo such awful punishment to reach it, I decided. It is a thought I cherish yet.

The blizzard raged throughout that night and all the next day, the drifts piling higher and higher. What amazed us was the wind, which continued to blow with the same speed it had had since the storm began. This caused nature to exhibit one of her most freakish phenomena for us. At the top of our hill, the wind picked up what appeared to be identical skiffs of snow and blew them at one even, unvarying velocity across the landscape—like an endless string of white dolls that a child might have cut out at the same time from many folds of paper. It was a fascinating sight, more so because it went on hour after hour.

We awoke on the third day to a quiet, windless world. No signs of life appeared anywhere on the vast sea of snow. It was as if man and beast had never been. No bruising footprint, no wounding hoof or paw had yet ravaged a virginal earth. It was an hour of serenity, as if an exhausted nature had spent herself on the blizzard and had pulled her white robes around her and lain down to rest.

But the slam of the kitchen door alerted the livestock and there was a chorus of whinnyings, bellowings, and squealings from the barns. In the henhouse, a rooster crowed welcome to the new day. Raucously cawing crows sailed in from the timber and settled in the topmost branches of the yard oaks, their sharp eyes watchful, their black bodies poised to swoop down instantly should a foolish field mouse skitter across the snow. A squirrel jumped down from a tree and floundered in the soft drifts. Our dog Queenie saw him and sprang into action, but her belly dragged and she couldn't get a foothold. The squirrel hopped and flopped his way back to the tree and shinnied up the trunk to safety.

All the paths that William had shoveled out the day before were drifted full again. He and all three boys, armed with shovels, swarmed over the earth like ants over a marshmallow and made new paths to the barns, the henhouse, the woodpile, and the Necessary. Only the top half of the windows on the north side of the house were visible. Snow was four to six feet on the level and William thought the drifts might be fifteen feet deep in the lane. We knew it would be several days before the snowplow would reach us. The telephone was still dead so our only contact with the world was through the radio. We were marooned in our own small Arctic.

Spurred by the cold, we developed appetites like bears coming out of hibernation. It takes a lot of food to feed five people three times a day and toward the last I had to improvise. When the pancake syrup gave out I boiled some brown sugar and water together and made more. We didn't like it as well but it served the purpose. We ate up the dry cereals very quickly and had to resort to oatmeal. I baked bread and cinnamon rolls twice but that used up almost all the flour. On the evening of the fifth day we sacrificed a fat hen and I used the last of the flour to make biscuits to serve with her rich gravy. There was canned food in the cave, of course, and plenty of milk, cream, and eggs. But we were, at that time, down to our last loaf of bread.

It was eight o'clock on the evening of the fifth day when we saw the lights of the snowplow shining over the drifts at the top of our hill. The plow was moving very slowly, like a tired dragon, chewing its way through the drifts and pushing the snow out to the sides of the road. Two hours later it rounded the turn into our house yard.

I watched it coming with both relief and regret. We had been snowbound before and we knew we would be again. We had learned to accept this, most of the time irked if not bored by our circumstances.

But this time it was different. After William and the boys' harrowing experience in the blizzard, we realized how lucky we were to be together again, and we had had a fairly long and not too unpleasant period in which to ponder our good fortune. The boys had enjoyed a brief vacation from school, and being snowed in had seemed like a break in the daily routine of our lives. Anyway, the world had gotten along without us—and we without it—for five whole days. None of us were all that eager to get back to it.

Raising a Family on the Farm

THE farm must surely be the best place in the world to bring up a family of children, especially if they are boys. They have acres and acres to play in and nobody cares how much noise they make. They don't have to worry about staying off other people's lawns nor throwing baseballs through other people's windows. There is always some kind of work they can do and they learn early in life that they can make a valuable contribution to the family welfare. Our three sons thought growing up on the farm was just great and they remember their childhood years fondly.

I remember those years with fondness, too, and like all mothers, it seemed to me that they went from coaster wagons to automobiles in the blink of a maternal eye. The intervening years were a time for hassling cuts, abrasions, black eyes, puncture wounds, measles, mumps, chicken pox, and colds. We had one bout with pneumonia (Jim) and one serious case of infection due to the jab of a ball point pen (Bill) and one severe penicillin reaction (Don), the latter after an ex-Army doctor had given him a shot directly over the heart, apparently oblivious to the fact that he was treating an eight year old instead of a marine.

I fear I did not possess the aplomb of Evalina, who had treated a severed artery with soap and sugar and had probably torn a strip off her petticoat for a bandage. Nor did I have the confidence in home remedies that my mother had had when she treated colds and flu by heating goose grease and turpentine together, smearing it all over our sore chests and covering it with a hot cloth. It was a treatment that served two generations well. However, I had no goose, therefore no goose grease. But I had Vicks and I still believed in the efficacy of the hot towel. And it was surprising what the lowly cake of soap would do. One time I accidentally stuck the tine of a dirty pitchfork into my ankle deep enough to hit the bone. William was gone with the car that day, so I couldn't get to a doctor for a tetanus shot. I washed the wound with hot soap suds and nothing happened — no swelling, no lockjaw.

It seemed to me that one of the boys was always having to get stitched up during those days. One day Don came home from school with blood running from a deep cut in his head. As I cleaned him up and assessed the damage, I asked him how it had happened.

"We were just playin'," he answered cautiously.

"Just playing? Playing with whom?" I asked.

"Oh, just a bunch of the kids on the way home from school. The kids that go our way. You know."

"What were you playing?"

"Oh, just playin'. Throwin' stuff around. You know."

"No, I don't know. What were you throwing?"

"Rocks."

"Rocks! How come the teacher didn't notice what you were doing?"

"She couldn't see us. We were down in the ditch. It wasn't her fault, anyway. We were off the school grounds. Teachers ain't 'sponsible when the kids are off the school ground," he said wisely.

"Who threw the rock that hit you?" I probed.

"I don't know. With all the kids throwin' rocks. . .how could I tell?"

I recognized his reticence in not wanting to rat on a classmate and I thought that was pretty good coming from a boy who wasn't old enough to pronounce the word "responsible" correctly. But this didn't alter the fact that he had several inches of skull exposed and had to be taken to the doctor to get sewed up. And I was 'sponsible for that, as well as a lot of other stitchings.

Bill once pulled the washing machine over on himself and got a bad cut on his head from the metal wringer. He was never able to give a satisfactory reason for upsetting the washing machine, but the time he pulled the metal kitchen cabinet over on himself he was only trying to get a cookie off the top shelf. I heard the fearful clatter of metal and breaking glass and ran to the kitchen to find him squirming under the debris. He got a nasty bump on the head and almost all the dishes got broken. The cabinet was never the same. He was also the one who impaled his finger under the needle of the sewing machine, causing the most painful cutting and stitching session at the doctor's that we ever had.

One time one of the two older boys swung a baseball bat around the corner of the barn and hit the other on the cheek, causing a bad bruise and black eye. To this day, there is some confusion about who did the swinging, and I have heard both of them claim the same black eye. But I can still remember with what eloquence the batter argued his case in court. How was he to know that his brother was coming around the corner at that exact moment? Besides, he was only practicing with the new bat, and if you were ever going to be a good ballplayer you had to practice, didn't you?

It does seem like I should be able to recall the identity of the culprit, especially since I was the judge who presided over juvenile court that day. But I can't remember. I can only explain this lapse by saying that it was just another one of those thank-God-it-wasn't-any-worse events that was promptly tucked away in this maternal mind and forgotten about.

Rural schools are now a thing of the past and I must say, frankly, that I think that is a pity. They had one big advantage in that they were close to our homes. The taxpayers could see first hand just how their money was being spent, and the parents didn't have to worry about those long and sometimes dangerous bus rides. We thought our children received as good an education in country school as they could have had anywhere, although there were obvious disadvantages in the areas of art and music. The library was always woefully inadequate, also, but books were available from the county superintendent and from the town library.

Most certainly, the students in a rural school were more likely to get individualized instruction. Nearly always there were older children who could help the younger children if they needed it. This made the older ones feel more important and the younger ones more secure. Quite frequently both benefited from this arrangement. There was something else, too. Hearing the older children recite day after day and year after year was bound to rub off on the younger ones. By the time they reached the eighth grade they had heard and studied a lot of history and geography and math.

Rural schools were established no more than four miles apart, so that no child had to go more than two miles to get there. Some schools had a well on the property but most of them didn't, so water was brought by one of the parents or carried in by the children from a nearby farm. Two Necessaries—one for the boys and one for the girls, set discreetly apart—were the only debasement of a large playground that was covered with native bluegrass for much of the year.

A small kindergarten student was always welcomed, taken in tow by the older children, and intitated into the realities of the school room and the joys of the playground. A rural school was just like a big family and, like any family, it was happier sometimes than others. Occasionally, a couple of the bigger boys would square off behind the woodshed and have it out with each other, almost always without the knowledge of their parents and the teacher. However, this often resulted in a sudden change in the pecking order and sometimes a better friendship between the two.

You would have thought that kids would never want to play hookey from such an interesting place, but Don and Bill and two other boys had different ideas on one occasion. The attractions of a warm spring day proved too much for them and they simply went down into a deep creek bed and stayed there until school was out. This deed would have gone undetected had it not been for one conscientious mother who was mystified to see that her son had been marked absent on his report card when she knew very well that he hadn't been. Her culprit confessed immediately, and she alerted the other mothers.

William had played hookey from country school in his younger days and he laughed it off as a harmless, boys-will-be-boys escapade. However, I pulled out all the maternal stops in an effort to make them see the error of their ways, including the threat that there was quicksand in the creek and they were taking their lives in their hands when they played there. The boys had no difficulty choosing between school and quicksand. They never played hookey again.

Once each year the students put on an evening program which usually coincided with the Thanksgiving or Christmas seasons. We listened attentively while impassioned Puritans reminded us of our heritage and we became silent and respectful when we beheld small angels draped in their mothers' best sheets, with the merest hint of a shined-up shoe peeping out from under. Any teacher worth her salt was expected to give one program each year. The kids, who had been practicing for weeks, were dead serious and anxious that everything went off without a hitch. Everybody for miles around came to the school programs. A lot of older people whose children were grown came because it brought back memories of their own youth. But mostly we went because the program was entertaining— and it was free.

Then there was always the potluck supper that followed and this was worth traveling miles for in any kind of weather. Every woman brought the best food she possibly could. She might serve a scorched loaf or a tough crust to her own family but what she brought to the potluck supper had to be perfect. Here her reputation was at stake. You could fool the men but you couldn't fool the other women. They knew! So when a woman took the white cloth off her basket and set her contribution on the long table you knew it represented her best efforts. If people came back for a second or third helping, or if one of the other women asked for her recipe, a look of satisfaction glowed on her face. This made all her work worthwhile.

And all we ever had to work with was "inconvenience" foods. Nothing ever came directly from a store or out of a box. Every pie, cake, salad, or casserole had been made from scratch and this was the way we wanted it. We did not begrudge a minute of the time we spent preparing for the potluck. The result was country cooking at its best.

Ah, those good old days! They are gone forever. Most schoolhouses have been sold and moved off to serve as grainbins or workshops. The playgrounds have been turned into cornfields. All that remains now are memories and those memories will be gone with the passing of another generation. Already the noisy, yellow buses roar by the places where the country schools used to be and there are no riders who can say, with pride, "That's where I used to go to school."

Regardless, there will be lots of us who remember the country school with pride and fondness. We feel sadness at the passing of an era and the loss of something that played such a vital part in our lives and the lives of our children. We still remember the satisfying contrast of white chalk on hard, black, genuine slate, still remember the earnest solemnity with which we took our places on the recitation bench, still remember the demanding clang of the old bell when it called us in from recess. As long as any of us live the country school will never really die.

Surely one of the greatest advantages in growing up on the farm lies in being able to keep pets without fear of bothering anyone else. We never had a cat after we moved to the old house at the end of the lane, maybe because we were so isolated that a stray cat couldn't find us. After our old terrier died I always said I wouldn't have another dog. However, that was before the boys got old enough to want one — and before Queenie came.

Abandoned because of her femaleness, she must have been booted out of a car somewhere in the country and finally found herself on the lane that led to our house. The boys were playing outdoors and saw her coming, skulking dejectedly, with her head down, her tail between her legs. She was a Collie, half-starved, her ribs plainly visible under her honey-colored coat.

She lay down in front of the boys, groveling, begging, her soft eyes pleading for acceptance. Our hearts went out to her. Rapport was easily established and a few pats on the head set her tail to wagging gratefully. Queenie no longer needed to grovel. She was "in."

And, as it turned out some weeks later, she was also pregnant. I will never forget the day her first puppies were born. I heard her scratching at the back door and went to see what she wanted. She was holding a limp, wet, mewling puppy in her mouth and she laid it at my feet with a well-now-you-know-what's-up look in her eyes. She waited until I had spoken a few consoling words and patted her head. Then she picked up her puppy and went back to the barn to finish her job.

Queenie was a terrific breeder but a lousy mother. She bore large litters but most of her puppies died soon after birth, victims of maternal neglect, we surmised, because she abandoned them almost at once and refused to go back so they could nurse.

The boys were always disappointed when the puppies died, but William was relieved. It saved us the trouble of having her "spaded," as Brick Nelson called it, and kept her from turning into a fat, useless creature without spunk enough to chase a rat or shake a bullsnake to death.

Although Queenie lacked maternal instinct, she did not lack intelligence. She guarded our door at night and always placed herself between "her" family and any stranger that came along. There was never any question about her devotion to us. It was as if she realized that we had saved her from starvation and given her a home and now she was paying us back.

There may have been times when I questioned the wisdom of living on the farm, but there has never been any doubt in the minds of our sons that the farm was the best place to grow up. Their lives may have been short on entertainment and long on work, but they learned to accept responsibility. We shared the good times and the bad times with no serious threat to the parent-child relationship, something I dare say might be envied by a great many families that are struggling to stay intact during these troubled days. And for this happy outcome we have the farm to thank.

Looking back across the years, my brother and sister and I still recall with sadness our last day on the farm. We seem to hear even yet the cries of the auctioneer that presaged the loss of our first home. We were too young then to understand why we had to go, and too young to fully appreciate what the loss of the farm had done to our parents. All we knew was that we had been happy there and we did not want to leave. We never really put down roots anywhere after that. We never really felt like we had a home anywhere we ever lived.

That did not happen to our sons. Because we never left the farm, they were spared the upheaval in their lives that I had known as a child. Regardless of what the farm did for us (and there were times when William and I thought it did very little), at least our children had a sense of belonging somewhere. And if asked about it today, they will still say that enabling them to grow up on a farm was the best thing we could have done for them.

Pure, Simple Catastrophes

THERE is one thing you have to remember if you farm and that is that you aren't going anywhere very fast. Nature herself takes care of this. She will not be hurried. It takes months for a sow to produce a litter of pigs and get them up to weaning size, months more before they are ready for market. No heifer ought to have her first calf before she is two years old, and from that time on she will produce only one calf each year. You will plant corn and soybeans in May, but it will be October before you know what these crops will yield, and there is no certainty then until every last kernel of corn and every last bean is safely in the bin.

Patience is one attribute a farmer must have in abundance, and waiting is the thing he must learn to do gracefully. Wait for the rains to come. Wait for the rains to stop. Wait for the corn to come up. Wait for the corn to ear. Wait for the ears to dry. Wait for the alfalfa to bloom. Wait for the little pigs to come. Wait for the calves to arrive. Wait...wait...wait, and be prepared to suffer financial losses, be prepared to sacrifice, be prepared to suffer catastrophes without losing courage.

I fear it is with a sort of perverse pleasure that I remember some of our very worst experiences on the farm. All these things did not happen in just one year, of course. If they had they would have done us in. Lumped together like this, they seem almost ludicrous. How could they all have happened? But they not only could happen—they did happen.

There was the time, for instance, when William bought a new hay rake and hay stacker on the theory that he had so much

William bought a new hay rake

hay to put up that he really needed something more than mere human power to do it with. Besides, he told me, there would be more hay than our own cattle could possibly eat, so he could sell some of it directly from the field and get enough money to pay for the machinery. There wouldn't be a lot of interest to pay at the bank this time. A short, thirty-day note would do it.

It seemed like a good idea and I gave him my blessing, not that it would have made any great difference if I hadn't, because I could tell he had his mind made up already. But it would make a lot of difference in the recriminations coming from the distaff side if the project failed, which, just as surely as God made little green apples, it was destined to do.

So the new rake and stacker were purchased with borrowed money, and brought home in time to use on the first cutting of hay in June. The weather was beautiful. A benevolent sun beamed down from a cloudless sky. All went well during the cutting, drying, and raking processes. Tons and tons of leafy green hay lay in the field only hours away from successful recovery.

Then overnight, the storm clouds gathered and early the next morning it began to rain, a hard, driving rain that soaked the hay from top to bottom. William was disgusted but not discouraged. It took more than one rain to ruin a hay crop, he said. When the sun came out the hay would dry on top, then he would turn it over and let the sun dry it on the bottom. The hay would lose a few leaves in the process but it would still be good, salable alfalfa.

But the sun did not come out and the clouds did not go away, or, if they did, there were others that blew in to take their places until it seemed like every cloud in the Western Hemisphere had made a pass over our hayfield. They showered, they rained, they poured. When they couldn't think of anything else to do they sprinkled — just so nobody forgot what water looked like.

Six days later the hay was a stinking, sodden mass, utterly ruined and useless. However, it had to be gotten off the ground so the next crop could come up. The same men who had been called on to help put up the hay came instead to help haul it to a ditch. It was a little like planning a wedding and having a funeral in its place. Now there was no money to pay for the rake and stacker, because the second and third cuttings of hay would have to be saved for our own cattle. Josh understood, he said, and we scrambled our priorities to include the debt on the machinery.

One spring we lost every baby pig we had, all because of some damnable new disease that the veterinarians had not seen before and didn't know how to treat. Of course, this would have to happen in a year when the mama pigs had outdone themselves and produced ten or eleven babies each, good by any standards. None of the pigs lived more than a few days and William carried them out by the bushel basket and buried them. We were advised to sell the sows because there was a strong chance that they might carry the disease on to future litters. We not only lost money but we lost a whole year's hog production and had to start all over again with a new herd.

One time William went to an auction of purebred sows, got carried away by the if-I-just-bid-another-dollar-I'll-get-'em psychology, and bought twelve. He paid almost twice as much as he would have paid for ordinary sows, but he was sure they were worth it, he told me when he got home. He had hired a truck to bring them out to the farm and I went down to watch them being unloaded.

They minced daintily down the loading ramp, formed themselves into a tight little group, and gazed snootily up at us out of marbly pig eyes. I got the impression that it was we—not they—who were being inspected. They really were beautiful animals. Their bristly black hides had been brushed to silken smoothness and they had real class, from their shining hooves to their velvety ears that were all gussied up with bright name tags. I had to admit that I had never seen any better examples of porcine pulchritude.

"But they don't look very piggy," I said, draping myself over the fence to get a better look.

"They'll have pigs all right. They're guaranteed," William told me.

"You paid too much for them," I accused.

"No, I didn't. They're worth every dime of it. Actually, they were a bargain, considering their background. They're all papered, you know. I could even sell breeding stock from them in a few years. That's why they all have names keyed to their ear tags—so I can mark their pigs and follow up on their bloodlines."

"Well, let's just hope they produce," I said doubtfully, still unwilling to concede.

"They will. I bet they all have big litters. Just wait and see."

We waited and, in due time, we saw.

Four pigs was the most any of the sows produced. Several produced only two or three and Bluebell birthed one, not much bigger than a runt at that. All the pigs were scrawny, unthrifty creatures that took their jolly good time about getting to market.

Pregnancies are terribly important on the farm. Every four-legged female on the place has to do her duty in order to keep you in business. But it always seemed to me that something that should have been pregnant wasn't and something that shouldn't have been was.

"The damndest things happen to us," William said one morning after we had just eaten breakfast.

"What's the matter now?" I asked, knowing from the look on his face that whatever it was, it wasn't good.

"I was looking at the heifers this morning before they went

179

to pasture and I believe most of them are pregnant."

"What's wrong with that?" I asked. "Think of all the calves we'll have."

"They're entirely too young to be calving, that's what's wrong with it. They won't be big enough when the calves come and they'll probably have a lot of trouble. I expect most of the calves will die and probably some of the heifers, too."

"Then again, maybe they won't. Maybe we'll be lucky for a change," I said.

"I don't think there's much chance of that," William replied gloomily. "Those heifers are just too young and too small to calve. I think we're in for trouble."

He had bought the heifers at auction and they were supposed to be "open," that is, not pregnant. He had intended to run them on pasture during the summer, let them clean up the stalk fields in the fall, and then fatten them on corn and alfalfa. But finding that they were pregnant knocked this scheme in the head. If sent to slaughter now, they would be heavily discounted. If they were taken back to be re-auctioned, we would almost have to give them away, because any farmer would have recognized them instantly for what they were—trouble on the hoof. All we could do was keep them and hope for the best.

William spent many anxious hours playing the role of midwife. He watched each heifer closely and when it became apparent that she was about to calve he shut her in the barn so she could be watched day and night. His worst fears were realized. Only a few of the heifers managed to produce live calves and almost all of those had to be forcibly pulled into the world. We called the vet several times but even then we couldn't save all the heifers. Eight of them died—a sickening financial loss to us—to say nothing of the suffering the poor heifers had to undergo.

I remember one heifer with painful clarity even yet. William worked with her for a long time but could not get the calf. I put in a hurried call to the vet but he was busy and could not come for a couple of hours. William kept on working but nothing he did seemed to help. It was awful to hear the sounds of such agonized bellowing coming from the barn and not be able to do anything about it. After the vet came, the bellowing became louder and more anguished for a time, then there was silence. My curiosity aroused, I went to the barn to see how things were going. The heifer was standing, still tied to the stanchion, the dead calf lying at her feet.

"Will the heifer live?" I asked.

"She will if she doesn't get infection," the vet answered. "I gave her a shot for that. But she's badly torn. She's in serious shape and may not make it."

He showed me just how badly she was injured and I understood then what tortures the poor heifer had had to endure. She died a couple of days later.

Not long after that I read a book written by a noted scientist, who asserted that there is no evidence of pain while giving birth in any creature except the human mother. His reasoning was that human mothers think, and they have been told that they will have pain, therefore they do have pain. According to his theory, it naturally followed then that animal mothers, who do not think, would not have pain.

That learned scientist was dead wrong, of course. Any farmer or farmer's wife can tell you that animal mothers do suffer and suffer horribly at times. With the injuries that this heifer had, how could she help but suffer? Furthermore, her bellowing was an expression of her pain. It is true that a cow usually calves very easily. She will go off by herself somewhere, lie down, strain a few times, and the calf will come. But it is not always that simple. What is supposed to be a natural function can become a life threatening situation very quickly.

Pigs are supposed to be intelligent and I cannot quarrel with that theory. One time we had a sow that was in labor much longer than she should have been. William had tried to pull her pigs but couldn't reach them. Finally, he came to the house to ask if I would help, saying that my smaller hand would be better. The sow was just lying there, grunting and straining at intervals. She lifted her head and looked at us and immediately her grunting changed to an I-know-you're-here-to-help-me tone. But I couldn't get her pigs, either, and she died later that day. Animal mothers that don't suffer? Don't you believe it.

Losing so many heifers and calves was a heavy financial loss and we had to use money from the sale of corn to pay back the bank. It was a classic case of robbing Peter to pay Paul. We had to do this many times. And sometimes Paul didn't get all that was coming to him because Peter didn't have all that much to rob.

Of course, we knew how the youthful heifers had gotten pregnant before they should have been. It can happen so easily. Any calf that is allowed to nurse its mother any time it wants to will grow at a fantastic rate. Organs that ordinarily develop much later will start pumping hormones into the calf's bloodstream long before she has attained full growth. Almost overnight a heifer will turn into a sloe-eyed beauty with amorous intentions that belie her tender age. If you dally one day too long in removing her from the presence of the herd bull, it will be too late. She will be pregnant months before her time. I still remember Ginger, to whom this very thing happened.

Ginger was a warm, spicy brown all over, except for a white spot in the middle of her forehead. She was allowed to follow her mother to pasture every day and so she had easy access to those plump pink spigots that were always filled with nourishing milk. Soon she weighed several hundred pounds and stood more than half as tall as her mother.

Late in the summer, Ginger's mother got into a let-em-eat-grass mood. Her calf was allowed to nurse only a minute or two and then her dam let fly with a well-aimed hoof and Ginger was kicked aside. Her mother would run a short distance away, ignoring her calf. It took awhile but Ginger finally got the idea: eat grass or starve. But no matter. Ginger had gotten off to such a good start that she continued to grow and stay physically far ahead of the less fortunate bucket-fed calves. But we waited too long to separate her from the other cattle and the bull, and by the time she should have been bred for the first time she was already showing calf.

Ginger carried her calf into late spring. William kept a wary eye on her but did not want to confine her until she was ready, he said. So each day she plodded out with the other cattle to eat the native bluegrass.

We should have known that nature, which had gotten the jump on Ginger once, might do it again. And she did. One evening the cattle came home without Ginger. William searched for her until dark and went out again the next morning. There were no signs of her anywhere. As a family, we converged on the timber and fanned out, covering almost every square foot of the pasture land. Still no Ginger. We inquired about her at our neighbors but no one had seen her. She seemed to have disappeared from the face of the earth. Obviously, she was dead, although William watched for months for traces of her hide or skeleton and found nothing.

Beset by birth pangs, had she wandered away in an effort to cope with the terrifying forces at work in her young body? Could she have been attacked by coyotes as she lay helpless giving birth? We would never know. Remembering Ginger makes me sad even now. She was such a pretty heifer and we had failed her. We had neglected to protect her from the consequences of her juvenile yearnings. We had been unwise and nature had been cruel, but it was poor Ginger who suffered for it all. In addition, her death represented a financial loss just as surely as if we had taken a hundred dollar bill out and burned it. Moreover, it would take two years to raise a replacement heifer.

One time William gave me a steer calf with the promise that I could sell him when he was grown and have all the money for myself. I don't suppose there was a calf anywhere that was watched with any more solicitude. I didn't know, of course, that he planned on committing suicide. One day he jumped the pasture fence into the alfalfa field. He ate and ate, and all those nasty little organisms that cause bloat began to grow in his paunch. When William found him he was dead, lying on his back, his belly swollen to twice its normal size.

To any cow, bull, or steer, the grass on the other side of the fence is always greener and infinitely more desirable than anything they can find inside the fence. They will go to great lengths to get it, even if this means breaking down the fence and maybe getting tangled up and cut in it. In fact there are any number of ways that unwitting bovines can get themselves in trouble—including sinking into mudholes, falling into ditches, and swallowing pieces of metal, like nails or staples.

Occasionally, a group of cattle will cluster under a tree during a storm—the worst thing they can possibly do, for if lightning strikes the tree it will kill several of them at once—or they may all spook and run, if lightning is close. However, if a storm doesn't amount to much they will go calmly about their business of browsing for food. It was during a light shower early in the day that we lost two heifers to lightning.

The storm was not a bad one and had not alarmed us or the cattle. There were some distant rumblings of thunder and the lightning had been needle thin, almost illusionary. Yet this kind of lightning can be very dangerous, as William discovered when he left the house after breakfast that morning. He found the two heifers lying dead, side by side, in the lane that led to the pasture. It wasn't hard to figure out what had happened They had seen some of that irresistible grass on the other side of the fence and had gotten down on their knees and stuck their heads under to get it at the exact moment that lightning coursed through the barbed wire. They were only a few feet from each other and they had died instantly, of course.

It seemed like such a terrible waste. We had raised them ourselves, had cared for them for two years and watched them grow. They would soon have had their first calves and showed great promise as milk cows. And now they were dead. It did not seem fair — either to them or to us.

It was during a storm a couple of years later when Dick, the dapple gray horse, was struck by lightning. William didn't know this for several days, however, until he called him to come to the barn. Dick took a few steps, stopped uncertainly, and whinnied. When William examined him he found that his legs and knee joints were stiffened and his beautiful eyes were cloudy and sightless. He lived out his days in idleness, his awareness of the world about him confined to the wind in his mane, and the snow under his feet in the winter and the warm sun on his back in the summer.

One of my most memorable experiences — which could have been much worse than it was — happened one summer at a time when the corn was looking exceptionally good and was already eared out. William was asked to stay overnight with a neighbor man whose family had to be gone and did not want to leave him alone because he had a serious heart condition. The man was even bigger than William, so it was a case of one giant baby-sitting another giant while the boys and I spent the night alone, even though there seemed to be a storm in the offing. I had agreed to this arrangement, however. I was sure that the neighbor needed William more than I did.

But the storm turned out to be one of the worst we had

had in years. The wind shivered the old house to its very foundations and the thunder boomed and crashed. Lightning struck a big tree about thirty-five feet from the house and split it from top to bottom like some gigantic axe, scattering limbs and throwing splinters almost two hundred feet away. The wind was so violent that I gathered my brood around me and held them tightly, afraid that the old house would come crashing down around us at any moment. Mercifully, it did not.

I told William when he came home the next morning that I thought we might have had a tornado. "Didn't you and Herman notice those awful-looking clouds?" I asked.

"No, we didn't even look," he said. "Herman just kept telling stories and bringing out the beer and sandwiches and..."

"Say no more. I get the idea," I said. "But I think you'd better look around because there may have been some damage."

He rode Muriel out to inspect the fields and found a wide swath of corn lying twisted and flat across the field directly north of the house. We had had a small tornado which, fortunately, had touched down about three hundred yards from the house. William thought the loss to the corn would be relatively small, probably not more than two or three hundred bushels, amounting to about six hundred dollars.

Any one of these events was a catastrophe, pure and simple, and I found it hard to see them in any other light. Occasionally, we did something foolish, like we had done with Ginger, and then we knew it was our own fault. But we weren't to blame when the lightning struck the heifers or when the rain spoiled our hay crop, nor when the baby pigs died from a disease that hadn't even been identified yet.

It was enough to make a pessimist out of anybody, and I was willing. William, however, was the eternal optimist who, if we had a bad spring, would look forward to fall, which he was sure would be better. Or if we had a bad fall, he would look forward to spring, which was naturally going to be better.

I fear I worked at being a pessimist in those days—partly because I was stubborn and argumentative and liked to play the devil's advocate and partly because so much cheerfulness in the face of disaster irked me. So every time William's optimism reared its ugly head I would chop it off instantly. If he rashly predicted the size of the corn crop I would tell him he had better cut those bushels in half. If he hopefully multiplied the number of baby pigs by the expected fall market price I would tell him that he had better wait until the pigs were in the truck and on their way to market before he multiplied anything by anything.

"You're always looking on the dark side," he told me once. "How come?"

"Because. One optimist in a family is enough," I said.

Actually, William was right. He took his lumps and came up smiling, which is the only way for a farmer to be. Hope is what keeps a farmer going, hope that next year will bring more pigs, more calves, more corn, better prices. In no one is the old adage "hope springs eternal in the human breast" better expressed than in a farmer.

There is no mystery in this, either. It is always possible that next year will be better, that production and prices will be good, and all will come together in one gloriously successful year that will put him on top financially. He will have the satisfaction of knowing that his struggle has been worthwhile, and he will feel that the land is where he belongs. It is this hope for the future that enables a farmer to persevere in the face of those unexpected difficulties — yes, even the catastrophes — over which he has no control. We persevered, too, not only because we had hope but because we both had a strong streak of stubbornness in us that would not let us give up.

But it must be remembered that all these events — the loss of the heifers, the baby pigs, the hay, and all the other things that happened to us — had their costs, not only in financial losses but in human costs as well. I do not remember now what I had planned on buying with the money from that steer who died eating the alfalfa. Whatever it was, I didn't get it. Nor were we the only ones to suffer such catastrophes. Many other farmers lost their baby pigs the same year that we lost ours, with the same heartache and the same blow to their pocketbooks.

It is all very fine to say that farmers walk hand in hand with nature, although they certainly do. Yet nature can be very cruel and capricious at times, and the ease and the speed with which she can turn on farmers is almost frightening. I suppose the thing we all dreaded the most was the hail storm, that could cut the corn leaves to ribbons or even cut the stalks off at the ground in a matter of minutes. And it happened to a few farmers every year. Nor did nature confine herself to the spectaculars of wind and cloud and lightning which, while they could fill us with fear and dread, could also give us something to marvel at. Nature could also pull any number of surprisingly murderous rabbits out of her seemingly never-empty hat.

I remember one spring when there was a bad infestation of chinch bugs. They were tiny insects but they could devastate a field in hours, eating every stalk of grain in their path. We knew they were working themselves our way but we didn't know when—or if—they would get there, so everybody was on the watch for them. One day I heard that long emergency ring on the telephone, and listened in to hear that the bugs were actually in the neighborhood. William and all the other men hurried over to help this beleaguered neighbor.

My memory as to exactly what they did to stop the chinch bugs is a bit hazy now. However, I think they dug shallow trenches around the edges of the fields and poured kerosene into the trenches, then beat the oncoming bugs to death with gunny sacks that had also been dipped in kerosene.

The battle was won before the bugs got to our fields, but our neighbor lost a considerable portion of his crop, for which there did not seem to be any insurance available. Fortunately, we had escaped this particular debacle. However, we had spent two or three weeks of glorious spring weather worrying about some little black bugs that propagated like crazy, crawled on the ground like a moving army, ate up every growing plant they came to—and after they had wreaked their havoc, zoomed away on the wings nature had given them.

I remember I had just baked cinnamon rolls that morning and had them frosted and ready to eat when William and Bob Irving came back from doing battle with the chinch bugs. Over coffee and warm rolls, we sat down at the kitchen table to talk about it.

"So many things beyond our control can happen, can't they?" I remarked. "It doesn't seem fair. Farming is such a big gamble. You never know how your crops are going to turn out nor how much money you're going to make. It makes me wonder why anybody wants to farm."

"Damned if I know," Bob said cheerfully.

And he was being honest about it. He really didn't know, he said. Couldn't understand what impelled a man to devote his whole life to something that was so unpredictable and, as far as money was concerned, often unrewarding. "I guess it's because most of us are gamblers at heart and we like to take chances," he finished.

"I think you may have hit the nail right on the head," I said.

My conviction, these many years later, is that Bob did indeed hit the nail on the head. Farming, like gambling, can get in one's blood. And there's just as big an element of chance in the turn of the furrow as there is in the flip of a card or a roll of the dice.

Farming — The Big Gamble

FARMING is the biggest gamble on earth. It has been so ever since the first scraggly-haired, club-swinging cave man carelessly threw some seeds on the ground only to be amazed some weeks later when he found young plants coming up. One can imagine with what excitement he pondered his discovery. So that was how he could get more food! All he had to do was throw some seeds on the ground and wait for them to grow!

Later on he must have realized that it wasn't all that simple. He must have noticed how important rain and sunshine were to his crops and, out of his fear and ignorance, probably spent many anxious hours on his knees propitiating the demanding gods of sun and cloud. Maybe if he pulled up some of his plants and offered them to the rain god the stubborn skies would open and the rain would fall? Or maybe the god of the sun would be pleased if he piled more rocks on his already towering altar?

The cave man must have developed a strong sense of ownership almost at once and he was no doubt incensed when birds or animals decimated his tiny garden. How could he protect this precious crop, this vital stuff that would keep his belly filled even when snow and ice had driven the animals to cover and he had no meat to eat?

He must have crept into his cave many nights pondering his dilemma. If he kept a fire going until sun-up, maybe he could scare the animals away. And if he got up at the break of dawn, maybe he could scare the birds off. He was the first farmer and he was already worrying. His twentieth century counterpart, albeit much less superstitious and much more scientific, is still worrying. The only difference now is that there is more to worry about.

That first farmer lived at a time when evolution (God, if you will) had caused the human forehead to bulge and the human mind to explode with additional millions of brain cells—and therefore ideas. Man had become a thinking animal. Even then, it must have taken him thousands of years to domesticate the pig and the cow, so that they could be herded along with him wherever he went and thus provide a continuing source of meat. Locating a kind of cereal grass, the heads of which would not shatter and fall on the ground when he harvested them with his hands, must have required the effort, time, and ingenuity of many generations.

It is possible that agriculture had its beginnings on the southern shores of the Caspian Sea, where the climate was mild, the soil rich, and the rainfall heavy. There Neolithic man found wild peaches, pears, apples, and grapes, as well as pheasant, ducks, geese, sheep, deer, goats, and the ancestor of the pig. The cow may have been domesticated from a dwarf race of ox that lived in the forests.

Man was still a wandering creature some eight or nine thousand years ago and did not stay in one place very long. But he must have left his cave for a more comfortable home made of mud and sticks and skins, and thus he had a feeling of belonging somewhere. Also, there must have come a time when his crops and his livestock were too valuable to leave unguarded, so he had to put down his roots for longer periods of time. Very probably this was the time in our history when wars began, for sooner or later a strange tribe would have wandered in and coveted what they saw. And what better way to get that land and those cattle and pigs and wattle huts than to kill for them?

But by freeing himself from the constant necessity for hunting and food gathering, man now had more time to think, to develop tools, to sharpen his verbal skills, to nurture and teach the young, and create some semblance of a stable society. Evidently it was farmers who launched mankind on the long road toward civilization.

Possession of land has been important from the earliest days of human history. Man has always been willing to sweat over it, to bend his back to it. And I like to think that those first farmers loved the land in their own simple way. They must have taken pride in it, been willing to fight and die for it. They must have thought that the land was good, that it would take care of them if they took care of it.

There have been harsh times in our world's history when land was owned by the favored few and reserved for their own selfish purposes. The ancient Egyptian farmer could never own land; he was only allowed to work it and give the proceeds to the Pharaoh. In France, not much more than two centuries ago, a man could be thrown into a dungeon for life because he dared to take a small animal to feed his hungry family from the hunting ground claimed by the king. As the world's population grew, land became much more scarce. The European peasant was lucky to have a few acres for himself, an amount similar in size to what we would put into a house garden or a lawn these days.

Small wonder then that the immigrants flocked to America by the millions in the eighteenth and nineteenth centuries. They were willing to leave their dear ones behind, make the dangerous sea crossings, work their way inward from the coasts, clear timber, and fight Indians — anything in order to get a few acres of that precious land.

The situation is not much different now than it was when those first immigrants arrived in this country. Land is still a precious commodity, and a man will gladly spend his whole life trying to pay for it. However, the value of land has risen many times over the years, and is now at an all time high.

During the 1880s my Grandfather Meier bought eighty acres in Northeastern Iowa for two thousand dollars. One acre of that land today would be worth almost as much as he paid for his whole farm. That virgin prairie that Grandfather Lightell paid a dollar and a quarter an acre for is now worth two to three thousand dollars an acre, not much more than a century later.

Incidentally, he once traded forty acres that Evalina had inherited for a gold watch and a setting of goose eggs. No doubt he did this because he already had land, and there was a limit to the amount of farming a man could do with oxen. Nevertheless, he had, in effect, killed the goose that laid the golden egg, because that land today would be worth about eighty thousand dollars. But how was he to know that? Those eggs, assuming that they all hatched, would have grown into fat geese and made several dinners for his large family. Anyway, a gold watch was considered a necessity as well as an adornment for a man in those days.

The bones of that ancient cave man have long since gone to dust; the only remaining evidence of his passage through this world lies in the flint tools that he left behind. By farming he had managed to elevate his living standards by the merest fraction, and by increasing his food supply he may have added to his longevity by a year or two. The only real sacrifice he had to make was some loss of freedom when he chose to settle down and stay in one place for a few months.

My grandparents and millions like them, however, had to make great sacrifices for the land. One can only imagine what back-breaking labor went into the plowing of virgin sod, what terrible hardships were worked upon a pioneer wife and mother, what deep loneliness must have possessed a farm family that lived miles and miles away from town and neighbors.

But farmers and their families are still making sacrifices for the land and will probably continue to do so. Part of this sacrifice lies in the nature of the work, which is unremitting and often dangerous. Machinery has taken much of the burden of manual labor off the farmer, but cows have to be milked, and livestock has to be tended no matter what the weather. There is always the chance for death or injury while operating machinery, especially when using it on hills or around ditches. However, the sacrifice that a farmer is most often called upon to make is financial. He is caught in a price squeeze that works both ways: everything he buys goes up while everything he sells goes down.

The trouble with farming can be expressed in one brief sentence: the farmer buys in a seller's market and sells in a buyer's market. The system works like this. When a farmer wants to buy a new tractor or a combine he goes to a retailer whose price will cover his costs plus a profit for himself. The farmer can either pay this price or leave the machine sitting there, go home, and make do with what he has. However, the farmer has no such advantage when he sells. A grain or livestock dealer will tell him to the penny what he will pay for corn, soybeans, wheat, hogs, or cattle. The farmer can either take this price or leave it.

He is in a better position to leave it if he is selling grain, because it can be stored and held in hope of higher prices. But the choice can not be made so easily if he is selling livestock. When his beeves are ready for market there isn't any point in keeping them around any longer, for they will only eat up a lot of expensive feed and the price can go down as well as up, in which case there is a double loss. And the longer a hog is fed the fatter it will get, resulting in a less desirable carcass that will bring less money per pound.

Part of the farm problem lies in overproduction, of course. The American farmer surpasses all other farmers in the world in productivity, an accomplishment that is at once his pride and his nemesis. Part of this is because this nation has been blessed with good soil, sufficient rainfall, and favorable growing conditions. The rest is due to the farmer's use of machinery, his unflagging ambition, and his desire to make some money. The result is a curse of overabundance, which causes depressed markets, and huge stocks in government storage, all of which put a heavy burden on the taxpayers.

My own opinion is that the difficulty lies, not in overproduction, but in underconsumption. If all the men, women, and children in America had all they wanted to eat, and if the unfortunate people of the poorer countries could receive enough food to keep them above the starvation level, there would not be any oversupply at all. Our surpluses would disappear as if by magic. This happy circumstance is not likely to come about — ever. But it is an intriguing thought.

The uncertainty about grain and livestock prices is only a part of the picture. Agriculture is always at the mercy of a capricious nature. Lack of rain at a crucial time will cut the grain yield by many bushels per acre. Too much rain, accompanied by cool and cloudy weather, will cause corn to be "soft" at maturity. Then it will quickly spoil in the bins without aeration or artificial drying. Hail, wind, and bugs can wreak havoc on a crop. There is seldom a perfect growing season, when sun and rain come at exactly the right time and the flying, crawling, and burrowing enemies are at a minimum.

Farmers, like everyone else, have also become very dependent upon others for goods and services. The cost of fertilizer, insecticides, herbicides, electricity, gas, oil, machinery, and seed have risen sharply. Yet these are all things they cannot do without.

One of my earliest memories is of my Grandfather Meier escorting us to his attic to see the seed corn that he had picked by hand. Grandfather had driven spikes through the rafter braces in his attic and had impaled each ear of corn on a spike. He was very proud of these big, yellow ears that he had chosen for length, symmetry, and the number of kernels in the butts. Of course, the corn was open pollinated and probably wouldn't produce half what hybrid corn will produce these days. But he had his seed all ready for the next spring and hadn't spent a dime out of pocket. The price of seed corn is now sixty dollars a bushel or more. What a change!

Electricity, once so cheap, has now become very expensive. Thirty years ago, when we lived in the house at the end of the lane, our monthly light bill was ten or twelve dollars. Today's farmer, if he uses heat lamps to keep his baby pigs warm in the winter, may have an electric bill of five or six hundred dollars a month.

We used to get fertilizer from the barn and it got pitched by hand into a spreader or wagon and hauled to the field by a team of horses. We have long since abandoned the horses (who, by the way, ate a lot of grain and thereby helped to dispose of surpluses) and we now buy our fertilizer in bulk, sacks or tanks and spread it on the fields with tractors that take a lot of expensive fuel.

Nor is bigger necessarily better, as many a farmer has found to his sorrow. During times when farmers are unable to recover the costs of production, they don't have to be Einsteins to figure out that the bigger the operation the more money they lose. Common sense dictates that there ought to be a solution to this and many other problems. Why shouldn't the farmer be able to recover his cost of production? Why should he have to take whatever is offered to him in the marketplace? Why is his share of the food dollar so distressingly small? Why does the wheat grower receive only one measly nickel from a loaf of bread costing a dollar? Why does the farmer have to be low man on the economic totem pole?

The answer, of course, is that this is the way it has always been and probably always will be. Agriculture represents free enterprise at its best — or at its worst — depending which side of the fence you are standing on. Farmers are forever condemned to buying in a seller's market and selling in a buyer's market. The alternatives to this system are unattractive, unworkable, and un-American. Controls imposed by government or by farmers themselves could help to reduce surpluses, thereby bringing up prices that farmers receive for their crops and livestock. They would also cause food prices to rise and place an additional burden on the backs of the poor.

So what is the future of agriculture? Will it continue to limp along from crisis to crisis? Or will it become the growth industry of the decade? And what about farmers themselves? Will they abandon agriculture in disgust or will they stay with it?

My guess is that a large percentage of them will stay with it. No matter what happens, farmers will continue to farm. They will do it because they love it and because they feel that they belong on the land. They would be unhappy without the feel of earth under their feet and the full sweep of skies over their heads. Most farmers are descendants of the peasants of Europe, whose sometimes unwilling but nonetheless determined blood still flows in their veins. They would feel like aliens working anywhere else.

Over a period of time, it is inevitable that some farmers will drown in the vast, uncharted seas of free enterprise. Yet that worrisome knowledge will not deter them from staying in agriculture as long as they can. Most of them are like the old farmer who was asked what he would do if he suddenly inherited a million dollars. He was silent for several moments while he pondered this intriguing question. Then he said, "Well, I reckon I'd just keep on farming until it was all gone."

A Time to Move On

WE could never tell with any degree of certainty when our relationship with the landlord began to sour, nor were we ever sure what caused this deterioration to take place. The chances are it was because of a lot of little things, sins both of commission and omission on our part, perhaps, that appeared unimportant to us but loomed large in his eyes. But the trouble began in our eleventh year on his farm and continued into the twelfth, when there were frequent rumblings from William that things between the two of them were not going too well.

It was a pity, really. We had started out with high hopes and much unity of purpose. Neither William nor I thought we'd ever have a farm of our own, but we were willing to work with the landlord so he could achieve his ambitions for his place. He had faith in us and we in him. He had confided his dreams to us and had given us the idea that we were important to him. Now there was a noticeable chilling in our relationship. He spent very little time working on the farm and did not even bother to talk with us when he was there. The conclusion we drew was disheartening and inescapable. We didn't belong on those four hundred hilly acres anymore. We were no longer a part of his dream.

We knew that it was time for us to move on, yet we made no effort that last summer to find another place. We would wait, we decided, until we knew for sure which direction the wind was blowing from. And we didn't find that out until the last possible day. There is a law in Iowa that requires a landlord to give notice by registered mail to any tenant farmer he intends to evict, and this must be done by a certain date. The fact that he had made us wait until the very last mail delivery was an indication of his feelings towards us, for he could have sent that letter months earlier had he chosen to do so. The long waiting period had been a sort of punishment for us, because it gave us more time in which to wonder if we would have to move and dread that we would. However, that registered letter, phrased in cold, hard, legalese and saying, in effect, "Move!" brought an end to our uncertainty. Now we knew what we had to do.

The neighbors had known about this for months, they told us. They rallied around us and gave us their sympathy and support, which helped us psychologically but did not solve the immediate problem of finding a place to move to. It was a year when there were more renters than farms and people were having to take any place they could get. William would have liked to get out of the hills, but there was little chance of that because all the bottomland was already rented. What few farms there were, were either undesirable or up for sale.

"You may have to buy a farm," Bee told me one day. "Sometimes that's the only way to get a place. Landlords can always find something wrong with a renter and it doesn't take much to make them move off. Why do you think we bought this place? It certainly wasn't because it's a good farm. But we had moved four times before we came here and we got to stay on the last place only one year. We decided we'd buy anything we could get our hands on just so we wouldn't have to move again."

It was a wonderful idea, but we knew that buying a farm now was an impossibility and would be for several years to come. Meanwhile there was much work to be done, and William plunged into the corn husking. We now had a small mechanical picker but the job required several weeks even then, and he did not get done until well after Thanksgiving. We had not found a farm by the first of the year and I was beginning to get a little desperate.

"What are we going to do?" I asked William one day. "We have less than sixty days to find a place and we aren't having any luck at all. We've got three kids to think about and we need a roof over our heads. We're going to have to make a decision soon."

William chewed his cigar thoughtfully. "I guess we'll just have to sell out and move to town," he said.

I flew into a veritable rage.

"Move to town!" I yelled. "I don't want to move to town! I want to stay in the country. I know the boys don't want to leave the farm, either, and I have no desire to raise three sons in town. Besides, you have no job."

"I'll find one," William answered.

"How? People don't find jobs just anywhere these days."

"You know, women are sure peculiar," William said. "You've been complaining all these years about how hard the work on the farm was. But when you get a chance to leave it, you won't do it. I wish you'd make up your mind."

William's calm acceptance of our predicament and his willingness to leave the farm was too much for me to bear, and I resorted to one of woman's oldest tricks. I cried. It moved him not one whit but it made me feel much better. Of course I had complained about the work, about having to carry all that water and live in such an old house, I told him. But I would have nothing except housework to do if we moved to town and I detested that more than I did the outdoors work. I liked living in the country, where our nearest neighbor was almost a mile away, and I would hate not being able to go outside without being watched, I went on. Not only that, but it would be awful to be without our own eggs and milk and meat. Sure, living on the farm was hard, I concluded, but we had a lot of advantages there that we wouldn't have in town.

William was understandably befuddled over my outburst and, when I had had time to think about it, I discovered that I was befuddled myself. I hadn't known that I was so passionately devoted to the farm. It was like thinking for years that you profoundly hated someone, only to find out much later that you actually loved the object of that hate. But at least our minor argument had the effect of clearing the air. William now knew where I stood on the subject of leaving the farm.

However, we were no closer to a solution to our problem than we had been the day the registered letter arrived, and time was running out. It was the middle of February when Bee called me one day, excited because she had found a farm advertised in the local paper. She read the ad to me over the phone. For rent,

373 acres, good cattle farm, plenty of water, modern house. Neither she nor I knew where the place was and we thought it must be a hill farm and probably not a very good one at that, otherwise it would have been rented long ago. But it sounded good to me, especially the part about the modern house. And we knew the owner, a fact that might give us some leverage.

I wasted no time thinking about it. I wouldn't have cared if the farm was so hilly that the cows had to crawl on all fours to get a mouthful of grass. For once it was people that counted, I decided. I called the owner immediately and asked if he had rented his farm yet.

"No, I haven't," he said. "Are you interested?"

"Yes, we are. William is gone this afternoon but he asked me to call you about it," I answered.

"I'll call back about seven this evening and we'll talk about it," he said.

I promised the owner, whose name was Emmet, that William would be there to take his call and I was ecstatic when I hung up the receiver. It had gone much better than I had dared to hope. True, I had told a small lie, but nobody needed to know about that. The important thing was to convince William that we ought not to let this opportunity slip by us. Perhaps I had overstepped my wifely bounds and gotten my husband into something of which he did not approve. But the worst he could do was berate me for my interference and reject the farm if it was offered, in which case the domestic fur was certain to fly.

However, I was apprehensive all that afternoon. I didn't know whether I should break the news to William early and give him some time to think it over, or wait until the last minute. I chose the cowardly way out. I decided I'd tell him just before it was time for the phone to ring. That way he'd have less time to marshal his defenses.

He came home and went directly to the barn to chore, while I busied myself cooking supper. From long experience, I had learned that the way to William's heart was through a baking powder biscuit, something I still detested to make. When he got baking powder biscuits without demanding and without asking there had to be a crisis in the offing, but I felt this was a crisis of no mean proportions. So I shoveled the cobs into Satan and while he was getting into the mood I mixed up a big batch of biscuits. I listened to the conversation at the supper table with half an ear that evening, still wondering what William would say when he found out what I had done.

When we had finished eating I plunged right in. "Why do you think you got biscuits for supper tonight?" I asked.

"You want something," he said.

"Not really. I did something today. And I don't think you're going to like it. I called Emmet and told him we wanted to rent his farm."

"You did!" William exclaimed. "But that place is so rough. It's nothing but hills, much steeper and harder to farm than anything we've had yet. I knew it was for rent all the time but I didn't want it."

"I know," I said soothingly, thinking to myself that the worst was over now. "The hills are bad. But you've always farmed them and one hill is pretty much like the next hill. This will probably be our last chance to get another place. It's Emmet's rough farm or nothing. He's going to call and talk to you about it."

"When?" William asked.

"In about five minutes," I replied.

There were long moments during that call when William was silent and I concluded that Emmet must have been explaining the terms of the lease to him. From William's short replies I couldn't tell whether they were acceptable or not. I studied his face, yet could get no idea what he was thinking. But sometime during that short conversation he must have said, "Yes." As he hung up the receiver he said, "Emmet is going to have the lease made out and he'll bring it up Saturday for me to sign."

I was overjoyed but I was careful not to gloat to William. No amount of biscuit making would atone for shrewish I-told-you-so's. I had gotten my way now. We weren't going to leave the farm and I was getting a modern house—the first in eighteen long years.

"Do you know who's living on Emmet's place now?" William asked.

"I don't know anybody who lives up that way," I said.

"Well, it's rather strange because the people who live there now are the ones who are coming here."

"So the renters are just swapping places."

"That's it," William said.

"Let us hope both landlords get a bargain," I remarked.

Neither of us women bothered to come and look at the house she was getting. It wouldn't have done us any good in either case. This didn't worry me at all. I felt sure that no matter what I got it would be better than what I had had for the last eighteen years. But I felt sorry for the other woman, who would be stepping down from a bathroom and running water to a Necessary and a pump that was quite capable of having one of its hundred-strokes-per-pail fits at any time, with all the inconvenience that accompanied both.

March first was supposed to be moving day for everybody. That was the date on which tenant farmers piled everything they owned into wagons or hayracks or trucks and scampered like so many rabbits to their new places. It was a little like playing musical chairs. It was sort of fun if you always found a chair. But sometimes you didn't get to sit on that chair more than a year or two and then you had to do the whole thing all over again. The miracle is that so many farm women have put up with this sort of thing for so many years without losing their sanity.

We had had much snow the winter before and spring was late that year. The snow was still melting and running off the hills in mid-March, making the roads on both ends nothing more than quagmires. So we couldn't move when we wanted to, and had to spend two weeks with the rugs rolled up and the curtains off the windows and boxes sitting around the floor.

But our wait was well worth it, and I was delighted when we finally got to the other house. Most of the rooms were large and there were lots of windows. The floors, except for the kitchen, were made of narrow oak boards and needed no rugs. The work space for cooking and dishwashing was nothing more than a converted pantry, but there was a window on the north and that miracle of miracles—hot and cold running water—in the sink. There wasn't enough room for Satan in the kitchen so we took him to the basement and I got a new electric stove.

The bathroom had a tiny lavatory tucked into one corner, a tub in which a full grown human could bathe, and a stool that would flush — we hoped — as soon as we got the septic tank and sewer pipes cleaned out. Fortunately, there was the usual back-up system, an aged Necessary sitting at a respectable distance from the house.

There were four bedrooms upstairs so each boy had a room of his own, and William and I took the largest bedroom with windows on the south and east. Something strange had happened to this bedroom. Although the other walls were all plastered and painted, our bedroom walls and ceiling were wainscoted. We surmised that it might have been a sleeping porch at one time and had simply been closed in the cheapest way possible. It also had a brick chimney along one wall, a hangover from the days when people had had a range in the kitchen below. But it was a pleasant room and I liked it.

There was a furnace in the basement that was supposed to heat the whole house. It didn't do an adequate job of heating, but we did not find that out until the next winter. But at least we no longer needed the two ugly stoves and they were taken to the workshop.

What I have described sounds very ordinary, and it really was. It was only because this house was so much better than anything we'd had for the past eighteen years that I was so happy with it. People kept telling me how old the house was, and it did date back to the First World War. But it didn't go back as far as the Indians went, so, to my way of thinking, it was relatively new.

While living on the other place we never got to see the mailman, but here he came to a box across the road. Don and Bill, who were both in high school by this time, had had to go almost two miles to catch the school bus when we lived at the end of the lane. Now the bus came past our very door. Jim, who was in the seventh grade, went to one of the last remaining rural schools, but it was only down the road and around the corner, much closer than the other school had been.

William was finding the farm more to his liking every day. There was plenty of hay ground and more than a hundred acres of pasture with two spring-fed creeks running through it. The outbuildings were more than adequate and a three-hundred-foot-deep driven well delivered water to the stock tanks and the house. We had a good windbreak of stately spruce, many black walnut trees, and acres and acres of oaks and elms. We were delighted to find that we also had five apple trees, one pear tree, and one plum tree.

The plum tree turned out to be sort of ridiculous. It was a young tree and had only a couple of dozen plums on it that first spring. One plum ripened each day. If I left it on the tree until late afternoon in the hope that there would be other ripe ones to put with it, I would find that the lone plum was already dotted with puffy bits of white mold. If I left it until the next morning, I would find it on the ground, all squishy and rotten with dozens of eager ants crawling all over it. For some reason or other, the little plum tree never did quite get it all together, and its performance did not improve with age.

There was nothing wrong with the apple trees, however. They burst into sweet smelling blooms very soon after we moved to the farm, and they bore lavishly. We had all the pies, sauce, and jelly we could eat, and gave apples to our friends and neighbors.

We felt very lucky indeed that we had managed to rent such a good place at what was, for us, practically the eleventh hour. However, there was a reason why Emmet's place hadn't been rented earlier. He had put almost all of it into what was known then as the soil bank — a government program that returned whole farms to idleness for long periods of time. The soil bank program was calculated to reduce crop surpluses, of course, and it did for a time. In return for idling the land both landlord and tenant received a check from the public coffers, a circumstance we found both helpful and galling, because we had never done it before.

In this case, Emmet got the lion's share of the money and we were left without enough farm land to do us any good. Almost all the place would do was keep the cattle herd going. We certainly couldn't live off our small government check and William was forced to get a job.

So what I had accomplished by my telephone call to Emmet that day had not been so great after all. True, we liked the new place and the conveniences that went with it. But what we had done was put ourselves in a sort of holding pattern until we rented another place or until the soil bank contract ran out—whichever came first. Meanwhile, we had to do the best we could.

However, our lives—especially mine—had improved immeasurably. For the first time since coming to the farm I felt like I was living in the twentieth century. I was happy in the way that only a woman who takes satisfaction from her family and home can be. And William, who had put up with me through all the bad years, thought it was about time.

Home at Last

MY bubble was soon burst. One morning about a month after we came to Emmet's farm a real estate agent appeared at my door. He had a thirtyish looking couple with him and he explained that the place was up for sale. Would I mind if these prospective buyers looked at the house?

My heart sank. Of course I minded, but I couldn't say so. I let them in and showed them around the house in silence, hoping that they wouldn't like it.

It was early morning and my beds were unmade. It was the only time in my life that I was ever thankful to have strangers catch me in such disarray, for there is nothing that detracts from the appearance of a room more than an unmade bed. And the master bedroom (I don't think that term had even been coined yet), looked the worst of all. I was using an old-fashioned comforter there, several pieces of which our ex-landlord had donated from some worn out trousers. It was a good, warm comforter, but it looked like something you would have found in a log cabin one hundred years ago. It did nothing for the room. I detected disdain on the woman's face when she saw it, and she was visibly shocked when she noticed the old brick chimney in a room where one would certainly never expect to see a brick chimney.

She didn't say whether she liked the house or not. Maybe she already had a better one, I told myself after they had gone. And I devoutly hoped that she did, more for my sake than hers, of course.

The agent brought no one else to look at the farm, but the

knowledge that it was up for sale was depressing. We knew that it would be sold eventually. Then where would we go? Back to another old house? Back to floors with splinters? Back to the tin washtub and the Necessary?

There were several difficult days during which my mood wavered between anger and despair. William was discouraged, too, but he was taking it a lot better than I was. We talked worriedly about the situation for a week or more, but neither of us could come up with a solution. I was uneasy because I never knew when the agent would bring someone else to look at the farm. Finally one day the idea came to me, an idea that was still hazy around the edges but sharply focused at the point of our problem.

"I've got it all figured out," I told William when he came home that evening. "We'll buy the farm ourselves."

"With what?" William asked.

"I don't know yet. But I'm going in to see Josh tomorrow. Maybe we can borrow the money for the down payment."

"I doubt that," William answered suspiciously.

"Well, it won't hurt to try," I said.

"No, it certainly won't hurt to try. But I don't think you'll get anywhere with Josh. You know how he is—he's sharp and cagey as hell. He'll find a dozen reasons why he can't lend you the money."

I sat across the desk from Josh that next morning and tried not to fidget under his stern gaze while I told him what I wanted. He said nothing until he had heard me out. Then it was his turn to talk, and he wasn't very impressed with my idea. He cautioned me with the kind of dogged pessimism that only bankers can evoke that there were probably a lot of angles to this proposition that I hadn't considered yet.

"Do you know what your principal payment would have to be each year? Or the rate of interest you would have to pay?" he asked.

"We've not talked to the real estate agent yet," I answered.

"How much are the taxes?"

"I don't know that, either. But I'll soon find out."

"The taxes on a place of that size are bound to be considerable," he remarked.

"I'm sure they are," I agreed, uncomfortably aware that I

was getting backed into a corner very quickly.

Neither of us said anything for several moments and I think that Josh was hoping I would just go away. But I didn't.

"I think we can handle it," I said bravely. "All we need is the money for a down payment."

"How much?" he asked.

I named a figure, give or take a couple of thousand. Josh went to his files and came back with a fat folder. He shuffled through the papers silently, then turned that Lincolnesque gaze on me again.

"You haven't got sufficient collateral for a loan of that size," he said. "Maybe in a year or two...."

"We can't wait that long. The place will be sold out from under us long before that," I answered.

"Well, I'm sorry, but I can't help you. And I must say I think you are taking a big risk. With almost all the land in the soil bank you won't have much corn to sell, and your government check won't cover the principal, interest, and taxes. I would advise you to wait a few years before you buy. There will be plenty of farms for sale later. Have patience. You're fairly young yet. You may find a better farm and a better bargain down the road." He must have sensed my disappointment because he added a few words, calculated to soothe, as I left the office. "That isn't much of a farm, you know," he said.

"Maybe not to you. But it is to us," I answered.

I had seen times when I liked Josh better. But it wasn't really his fault that we lacked collateral, and I hadn't handled the situation very well, either. I simply hadn't had all my ducks in a row when I went to the bank. I made up my mind I'd have to do better when I talked to the real estate agent. Because I was determined not to give up yet, not until we had exhausted all possible avenues of approach. I called the agent and arranged a Saturday appointment, when William would be home.

"Maybe we can make some kind of a deal with Emmet," I told William that evening.

"I doubt that. He will probably want a big down payment and, besides, he may be asking more for the farm than it's worth. We've got to be realistic. I think you had better brace yourself for another disappointment." William cautioned.

But we hadn't considered Emmet's feelings towards us, nor

did we know what was happening in his life at that time. He was gravely ill, the agent said, and wanted to get his financial affairs in order. "I'm sure he thinks he doesn't have much time left. He likes you folks and wants you to have the place, and he's got a deal worked out that he hopes you can handle."

So we sat down at the kitchen table while the agent explained what Emmet could and would do. Because it was not yet the first of May, whoever bought the place now would get all the crops and all the soil bank money. The government check would make a sufficient down payment and Emmet would agree to wait for his money until that check came. The price per acre was reasonable and the interest would be five per cent. There would be a principal payment of two thousand dollars a year for the first five years, then it would drop to one thousand.

We could scarcely believe our ears. All our worries evaporated like dew on a warm morning. We didn't need Josh or anybody else. The only thing we needed now was a few hundred dollars earnest money. We had that—and God knows we were earnest enough.

I don't suppose there were ever any two people who signed their names on the dotted line so fast. I do not remember where the boys were when this great event in our lives took place. But my recollection is that they were not there. They may have been working for a neighbor (growing boys are always in demand on a farm), or they may have chosen not to be around to see our disappointment if we were turned down. But they were as delighted as we were when they finally got the news.

We had, however, put ourselves in a rather precarious position and we knew that. We had bought on a land contract and if we missed our first-of-March payment by as much as thirty days we could lose the farm and everything we had put into it. We simply couldn't allow that to happen, we told ourselves.

"Home at last!" I said to William that evening when we were sitting on the porch contemplating the day's events.

"Yes, it's a great feeling," William said, puffing contentedly on his cigar.

"But we've got some rough times ahead of us. We're going to be in debt for the next thirty years. Have you thought about how old we'll be when this place is paid for?" I asked.

"Old enough to die, I guess."

"But we're still quite young. We ought to be thinking about living—not dying. And now we can do some of the things we want to do instead of what somebody else tells us to do," I said.

We sat on the porch a long time that evening, each of us talking about our plans for the farm. William, usually not much of a talker, was really fired up. Tomorrow he would start cutting fence posts from the timber, he said, so he could repair the pasture fence. Then he would put some new partitions in the hoghouse, using some lumber that a previous tenant had left in the barn. Later on, he would have to brace up a corncrib that was beginning to lean. For this he would have to have some help from the distaff side. I promised my help gladly. If he had said he needed a good mule I expect I would have volunteered.

"There are a lot of improvements I can make around the place without spending a dime," he finished.

We made one improvement very quickly. We pulled the Necessary down. I don't know of anything we did in those first few days that gave me any more satisfaction. Seeing that hated symbol of poverty and backwoodsiness get hauled off didn't quite compensate for the thirty-nine thousand, four hundred and twenty trips I figured I had made to it in my day, but it certainly did a lot for my ego. It put us on a par with the rest of the world.

Although there was some good bottomland on the place, there were many hogback hills that were good for nothing except pasture. One day Don, who was eighteen then, drove Muriel out to inspect a fenceline. Despite all attempts to rein Muriel in, she rolled down off one steep hill so fast that he had trouble getting her stopped when they got to the bottom. He came into the house thoroughly disgusted.

"I wouldn't have this place if you'd give it to me," he declared hotly.

"That's because you're young and you don't understand yet how hard it is for people to get their hands on a piece of land," I replied.

There were many times when William and I thought we'd never make it—couldn't see how we could possibly come up with our yearly payment. The first of March became a fateful day for us; it hung over our heads like the sword of Damocles.

Those were the times that I thought of my father's heartbreak when he had lost his farm, and I could more fully understand now how he had suffered. But we always managed to come up with the money somehow, and Josh helped us more than once with a thousand or two. He really wasn't taking much risk in doing this because land had begun to appreciate in value very soon after we bought the farm, and each year it was worth more than it was the year before.

Womanlike, I had great ambitions for the house. I would modernize the kitchen, put a picture window in the dining room, and maybe knock out a couple of walls to make an L-shaped living room with a fireplace at one end. Of course, we didn't have the money to do any of these things. But it was a nice dream and it sustained me through the years when the furnace kept blowing up, the bugs ate off the alfalfa, three precious cows sank to their deaths in the ordinarily trustworthy creek, the taxes more than doubled, the two older boys decided they wanted to go to college and we knew that somehow we must help them.

Tradition has it that farmers live poor and die rich. Or is it the other way around? Certainly, there is much in farm living that cannot be measured in dollars. William and I had so many years during which the struggle to pay for the farm threatened our pleasure in living there. Yet there were compensations even then.

When I would see the miracle of the rising sun, seemingly balanced on edge for a few seconds on the top of our pasture hill—then I knew a joy far beyond anything money could buy. When the hillsides were dotted with little calves and I saw with what loving wariness they were guarded by their four-legged baby-sitters, then my heart swelled with pride, for those creatures were beautiful in my eyes. When I saw the pheasant rooster strutting in iridescent splendor along the creek bank and could hear the high, clear keening of his call—then I knew how lucky I was. I wished that everyone could see and hear him. And when we saw a small herd of deer leisurely ambling along as if our fields and our timbers were home to them, then I knew that we were not poor at all. We were rich in all the ways that really counted.

Don and Bill, after trying several other kinds of work, have come back to the land. Jim, who never left the farm at all, is living on the home place now. I like that phrase "home place." It has a fine ring to it. It embodies so many worthwhile concepts: family and love and purpose and continuity. The home place is a part of growing up and, inevitably, a part of growing old.

So our sons represent the fifth generation of farmers in one family. However, these are only the generations we know about. There must have been many others that preceded us, generations about whom nothing is remembered now. Even so, we have a line that spans almost a century and a half—from my mother's ancestors, who plowed the virgin prairie with oxen—to our sons, who roar across the fields driving high-powered machines. There is a continuity with that family line, an identification with those who have gone before.

Yet we play only a minor role in the great drama of mankind, for today's farmer is merely the latest tiller-of-the-soil to come on the stage. We were preceded by many millions of others, from the ancient hunter-gatherers, who gave up their wandering ways and went to grain growing, to those toiling peasants of Europe, to those daring immigrants who risked their lives to come to a strange country in search of land. That makes us a part of history, and it is good to be a part of such an enduring and honorable history.

The memory of that April morning when William and I loaded our belongings into a hayrack and moved to the farm is still clear in my mind. There were many times in my life when I thought the bull that we took by the horns that day was the biggest, ugliest, meanest, most cantankerous bull that anybody could possibly have chosen for an adversary. But most of the time we managed to throw him, and if he stood up again and glared at us—we didn't run. We glared right back. And I am almost certain I would take hold of those same horns again. I will never forget the hard work nor the worry nor the high hopes that so often ended in disappointment. But I count our blessings, too, and I will always remember the times when things did go right, when we could look back and say to ourselves, with satisfaction, "We had a good year."